A City of Palaces

Bath through the eyes of
Fanny Burney

by

Maggie Lane

Millstream Books

To all my friends in the Burney Society
on both sides of the Atlantic

First published in 1999 by
Millstream Books, 18 The Tyning, Bath BA2 6AL

Set in Palatino and printed in Great Britain by
The Matthews Wright Press, Chard, Somerset

© Maggie Lane 1999

ISBN 0948975539

British Library Cataloguing-in-Publication Data: a catalogue
record for this book is available from the British Library

Contents

Acknowledgements

My thanks are due to the Oxford University Press and to the Burney Project at McGill University for permission to quote from the letters and diaries of Fanny Burney.

I would like to record my personal thanks to Jean Bowden, for inviting me to give the talk from which this book grew; to Kate Chisholm and Karin Fernald, for an afternoon hunting d'Arblay memorials at St Swithin's; to Stuart Cooke, for electronic transmission of text from McGill University, Montreal; to Rupert Lane, for doing the business in New York; and to David Selwyn, for supply of books beyond the call of friendship. I am especially grateful to Rachel Brodie of the Beaverbrook Art Gallery and Charles Noble of Chatsworth House for help with the portraits in their keeping, and to Tim Graham for being a publisher with whom it is a pleasure to work.

Introduction

The novelist, playwright and diarist Fanny Burney lived to a very old age and thus saw immense changes during her lifetime. When she was born in 1752 George II was on the throne; when she died, aged 87, in January 1840, his great-great-granddaughter Victoria was Queen. Fanny began life 23 years before her famous successor Jane Austen, yet outlived her by a further 23 years.

Fanny Burney not only lived through great changes in the social and material fabric of Britain: she recorded them. She was an inveterate diary-keeper and letter-writer all her life. Her private papers, amounting to some ten thousand manuscript pages, are becoming increasingly valued as a resource for historians investigating many diverse topics. The record she has left us is invaluable both for its minute and lively observation of people and places over such a length of time, and for its rare female perspective.

Fanny Burney was a woman with a woman's interests and outlook; but unlike the vast majority of women of her period, her opportunities for observation were not confined within a narrow domestic sphere. Her father's profession and friendships among the artistic community of 18th-century London, her own literary fame, the strange chances of a life which swept her at one time to immurement at the court of George III and at another to exile in Napoleonic France, made hers as eventful and changeful an existence as a woman could well experience. And through everything that befell her, she kept on writing. Not only four substantial novels and several plays, but private diaries, long journal-letters to her sister Susan and others retailing her doings day-by-day, and accounts of certain key episodes in her life compiled years after the events described. For Fanny, it would seem, as for Virginia Woolf, no experience was fully lived until it had been put down on paper.

Fascinating though this vast body of writing assuredly is, its sheer quantity (more than 20 published volumes) can be daunting to a reader interested in a particular topic or theme. It is with just such a reader in mind that I have drawn together all Fanny

Burney's writings on Bath, setting them in the context of a chronological account of her connections with the city. The aim is to provide an accessible and focused picture of Bath as experienced by one woman over a period of time.

Fanny Burney's knowledge of Bath spanned half a century, from her first visit in 1767 to her farewell to the city in 1818. Even after that date, she continued to correspond with sisters living in Bath right up until her own death in 1840, thereby following at one remove the continued physical expansion and social decline of the city she knew so well. Fanny's writing on the subject includes not only passages of great immediacy, with the power to make us feel we are there with her in 18th- or early 19th-century Bath, but also occasional reflections of a forward-looking or retrospective nature, which she was well qualified to make.

Besides being a chronicler of social changes, she exemplified some of them herself. In 1780 she was one of the illustrious people from the world of arts and letters who flocked to Bath for recreation almost as a matter of course. Thirty-five years later she and her ailing, penurious husband chose the city for their retirement, Bath having transformed itself in the interim from a resort for the fashionable into an economical yet still agreeable place of residence for the impoverished gentry.

For unlike Jane Austen (whose parents also retired to Bath on a small income, bringing their reluctant daughters with them), Fanny Burney was very fond of Bath. She appreciated that blend of town and country amenities in small compass which was its unique contribution to civilised living. Inevitably she very often saw things to criticise or ridicule in the goings-on there, but as a keen observer of human behaviour she found much to stimulate and interest her. Fanny never returned to Bath after a lengthy absence without expressing spontaneous praise of its beauties, both architectural and natural. As she grew older and the place grew larger and more staid she seemed only to like it better; her eventual residence there was a matter of great satisfaction to her, and when she left after her husband's death it was with none of Jane Austen's 'happy feelings of escape'.

There is, therefore, a sparkle about her writing on the subject of Bath which has long assured her a place in any anthology of impressions of the city by its famous visitors. These brief extracts are enjoyable but they are only a fraction of what she wrote on the subject and, stripped of their context, they can give little idea of the personality or background of the woman who wrote them. The time has come for a more sustained look at Bath through the eyes of Fanny Burney.

* * *

The modern writer on Fanny Burney has decisions to be made regarding nomenclature. Americans especially object to the diminutive Fanny, feeling that it infantilises and patronises her. They point out that she never published under that name (in fact her first novel was published anonymously, and her subsequent ones as 'by the author of *Evelina'*) and that although she was unquestionably known as Fanny in the family circle, it was only when the Victorians started to write about her, in their somewhat cosy way, that she was presented to the public as Fanny Burney. From the time of her marriage her legal name, and the one she always used herself, was Madame d'Arblay (proud of her French husband, Fanny corrected anyone who called her Mrs), but this is equally unacceptable to those of a feminist persuasion, and it certainly does not convey the writer known to us today.

In America the preference now is for Frances Burney (a name she was never known by in life) or, in academic writing, just Burney. The Burney Society was the name chosen, in a somewhat uneasy compromise, by those of us who in the early 1990s founded, simultaneously on both sides of the Atlantic, a Society to further understanding and appreciation of her life and work. In this book, however, she will appear under the name familiar to most British people, the name with which she is commemorated on the plaque at 14 South Parade, Bath: Fanny Burney. My justification, if any is needed, comes in her exuberant private journal entry for 1778: 'This year was ushered in by a grand & most important event, – for, at the latter end of January, the literary world was favoured with the first publication of the ingenious, learned & most profound Fanny Burney!' So that was how she thought of herself, even as a published writer.

In Chapters 4 and 5, a similar problem presents itself: how to refer to her husband. His name was Alexandre d'Arblay, but his

Christian name is rarely seen in the extant writings. In addressing him directly Fanny invariably made use of some endearment, while in referring to him she would write 'M.d'A'. A recent biographer has adopted this abbreviation throughout her book, but that looks rather odd to me, and M. d'Arblay seems too formal an address, and too awkward visually, for my purposes. In this book therefore he will be given back his name and known as Alexandre. Their son, who bore the English spelling of the same name, was always known as Alex, so there is no problem in distinguishing between the two men in Fanny's household.

Finally a note about transcription. For ease of reading I have silently brought the 18th-century fondness for capital letters into line with modern usage. I have felt justified in expanding abbreviations made with no other purpose than to facilitate writing at length and at speed: had the manuscript been sent for typesetting at the time it was written, any contemporary printer would have been expected to do the same. However, use of the ampersand and original punctuation have been retained, reflecting as they do the character of letters and diary entries dashed off in haste, without obtruding themselves unduly on the modern eye. Scholars seeking a completely literal transcription are referred to the published letters and journals (see the Bibliography), from which all quotations are taken.

1. Fanny Burney, Her Family & Fame

Charles Burney

Among the fashionable arrivals recorded in the *Bath Journal* of 2nd November 1747 was Mr Fulke Greville, whose country seat was Wilbury in Wiltshire. Young, unmarried, dilettante and rich, Greville was able to indulge every whim, a recent example being the acquisition of a resident musician as part of his household. Requiring somebody who could converse on the level of a gentleman yet who was thoroughly proficient in music, he had for some time despaired of finding the right person. Most professional musicians were not sufficiently well-bred for him to tolerate their company; few gentlemen had the incentive to apply themselves to music like a professional, and in any case would not have wanted to be at another's command. But in the summer of 1746 Greville had found what he was looking for in Charles Burney, a 20-year-old apprentice to the London composer Thomas Arne.[1]

Charles came from a good family which had fallen on hard times, being with his twin sister the 19th and 20th children of an improvident father who had so alienated his own father that he had been disinherited and obliged to seek his living on the stage. Many of the surviving children were musical, none more so than Charles. He played every kind of instrument, he composed, he impressed everybody with his understanding of music from an early age; in his maturity he was to write a history of western music that stood as the authority on the subject until modern times, to be honoured with a doctorate and finally to be memorialised in Westminster Abbey. He had inherited talent, charm and easy manners from his father, to which he added what his father so conspicuously lacked, application, prudence and a desire to better himself. For many years the young Charles Burney made it a rule never to go to bed without having learnt something which he had not known when he rose in the morning. Having suffered from the lack of both during his childhood, the twin quests throughout the course of his life were social respectability and family solidarity.

[1] Lonsdale, Roger, *Dr Charles Burney, a Literary Biography*, OUP, 1965.

Greville bought out the remainder of the apprenticeship from Arne and took Charles to live with him at Wilbury, where he occupied a strange position, an employee, yet on familiar terms, always dining at Greville's table. In an age of patronage, the contacts that Charles made among Greville's associates were to stand him in good stead. Charles accompanied Greville everywhere, including to Bath.

At this point in its history, Bath was the haunt of the aristocracy, and gaming the chief occupation of their evenings. An Act of Parliament of 1739 had attempted to curb the habit by making games of chance 'with numbers thereon' illegal. To get round this, the Master of Ceremonies Beau Nash, who had helped make the city the fashionable place it was, and in the process made himself a fortune at the gambling tables, introduced the new game EO, standing for even and odd.

Charles Burney witnessed the hold that this game had over the company at Bath. His other memories of their three-month stay in the city, written down many years later, were of its then sparse musical life. Thomas Chilcot was the organist at Bath Abbey from 1733 to 1766; Thomas Linley, at the time of Charles's visit a boy of 14, was to become the eminent Bath musician whose famous singer daughter Elizabeth eloped from their home in the Royal Crescent with the Irish playwright Richard Brinsley Sheridan. This is what Charles Burney recorded of Bath in 1747:

> Here I got great credit by playing Scarlatti lessons to Lord Holdernesse, Lord Cowper, & the two Mr Franks, passionately fond of music. A bad old harpsichord was hired of Chilcot organist of the Abbey; Linley was then his apprentice.
>
> I saw the humours of high, or rather deep, play at hazard, & the private EO table; Duke Hamilton, Lord Chesterfield, Lord Waldgrave, Lord Montford, Sir Hugh Smithson, Mr Greville &c were usually of these parties. Guineas were there in plenty, bank notes but few. I have seen 1000 guineas in one heap, and Lord Holdernesse tired of winning small sums cried out … 2 or 3 professed gamesters clubbed stakes and eased his Lordship very soon of his golden incumbrance.

The chief music at Bath was now at the Pump-room of a morning; I can remember no evening concerts, nor any other music in the ballrooms than minuets and country dances. I saw the tyranny of the Master of Ceremonies Beau Nash, with his white hat under his arm and open breast, the coldest day in winter; I used to get up early in Pierpont Street to see the great Lord Bolinbroke carried in a chair to the Pump-room for privacy, before the rest of the company was assembled.[1]

From Bath, Greville and Charles travelled to London, where shortly afterwards Greville eloped with the heiress Frances Macartney (just to add spice to the marriage; there was no opposition from her family), asking Charles to give the bride away. Charles, who instructed her in music, called her 'the beautiful, charming & accomplished Mrs Greville', adding that her 'counsel, conversation & love of literature' helped to form his character and make his position at Wilbury even more congenial than it had been before. The Grevilles were to remain friendly and useful to Charles all their lives; it was in honour of Mrs Greville that his second daughter acquired her name.

The Young Burneys

Meanwhile Charles himself was becoming romantically entangled with another lovely and musically accomplished young woman, Esther Sleepe, daughter of the leader of the Lord Mayor of London's band. On 24th May 1749 Esther, as yet unmarried, gave birth to a daughter, another Esther, usually called Hetty in the family. The Grevilles were on the point of leaving for a protracted tour of Italy, expecting Charles to go with them. It is inconceivable that he did not yearn to visit the country whose music he was to love and study all his life; Esther still generously urged him to do so, despite the fact that the Grevilles were planning to be away several years. She even had her miniature painted, that Charles might carry it about and not forget

[1] Klima, Slava et al, editors, *Memoirs of Dr Charles Burney 1726-1769*, Nebraska University Press, 1988.

her. But whether from love or conscience, at the last minute Charles confessed Esther's plight, obtained Greville's blessing, and married her on 25th June. Little Hetty was baptised the same day.

Charles now set about making a living as a music teacher, church organist, and part-time musician at Drury Lane theatre. He also published some of his own compositions. The contacts he had made through Greville proved useful and he found himself mixing with the nobility as well as with the famous writers, painters and actors of the day.

Two sons were born in quick succession, and Charles was beginning to make a name for himself, when ill health, perhaps brought on by overwork, threatened to cut short a promising career.

Advised that he must leave London, Charles obtained the post of organist at St Margaret's church in King's Lynn, Norfolk, where on 13th June 1752 – days short of his third wedding anniversary – his fourth child and second daughter was born. She was named Frances after her godmother Mrs Greville, but always known as Fanny in the family.

Small in size, timid in demeanour, and exceptionally slow to learn to read, she attracted no particular notice in the nursery. Neither the eldest nor the youngest, she was besides not musical, like Hetty and like Susan, the sister who came after her; she was not a precious boy (the Burneys buried three infant sons in King's Lynn); her health did not give particular cause for concern, as Susan's often did. Fanny's talents were for observation, verbal retention and mimicry, but it was some time before they became apparent. Charles, always avid for the credit of his family, had no suspicion, until *Evelina* burst on the world, that it was his shy, retiring daughter Fanny who would do most for the name of Burney.

The Burneys were nine years in Norfolk. In addition to his work as organist, Charles gave music lessons at the great houses, often staying on to dine. Ever anxious to make good use of every moment, he taught himself Italian while riding to engagements on horseback, carrying a volume of Italian poetry in one pocket, and in the other an Italian dictionary that he had written out himself. To ward off 'professional rust', as he called it, and to keep up with his acquaintances, he visited London for a month every winter. It was during one of these visits, early in 1758, that he first met Dr Johnson, who was to become a fond admirer of both Charles and, much later, Fanny. Indeed he loved 'all the dear Burneys, little and great', and said that he loved them all the better because they loved one another so well.

By 1760 Charles felt ready to return to London with Esther and their surviving children, Hetty, James, Fanny, Susan and Charles. Hetty had by now begun to perform publicly and with great precocity on the harpsichord, a good advertisement for her father's teaching methods as he re-established his professional life in London.

His health had fully recovered, and he would live on to his 88th year. Esther was not so fortunate. As her ninth pregnancy in twelve years progressed, she began to show symptoms of consumption, and was ordered to take the waters at the Bristol Hotwells, where Charles joined her for a month in the summer of 1761. Charlotte was born that November, and in the following September Esther died. In the final days of her illness the youngest children were looked after by a neighbour, who said she had never seen a child cry so inconsolably as did ten-year-old Fanny when she was told the news.

Fanny's first visit to Bath

Despite her slowness in learning to read, soon after her mother's death Fanny began to find solace in writing. By her 15th birthday she had accumulated sufficient manuscript pages – including a complete novel – to make a very respectable bonfire. The reason she destroyed all her writing to date was not because she was ashamed of its childishness, and was ready to move on to something she could be more proud of, but because she had been made to feel guilty about indulging in this private pleasure at all. The person making her feel guilty was the woman who was about to become her father's second wife, Mrs Allen, the widow of a King's Lynn merchant, with whom Charles had been in love since 1764.

The marriage was delayed because of opposition from her family, who thought a poor music teacher not good enough for her. In the summer of 1767, within weeks of Fanny's bonfire, Charles resolved to visit Mrs Allen's brother at Bristol Hotwells in an attempt to bring him round to the match, and he took Fanny with him for company. On the way back to London they stopped in Bath.

Charles certainly had reason to be distracted on that journey, what with anxiety about his new marriage and memories of his old one, for only six years earlier he had been at Hotwells with the desperately ill Esther. We can imagine Fanny as a quiet but sympathetic companion, honoured to be singled out and given this opportunity to serve her father – perhaps the first time he had really got to know her as an individual. The halt in Bath may have been made for her benefit, to give her pleasure and a little more knowledge of the world; or it may have been designed to bring Charles himself some relief, reminding him of his carefree youth in Bath with Fulke Greville, 20 years before. Despite the passage of time, he probably still had acquaintances there.

Unfortunately we know nothing of the visit, its duration or where the Burneys stayed. If Fanny recorded her impressions of the city at the time they are lost to us. What is certain is that it was not until March of the following year that she began to keep her private diary. This first visit to Bath took place in the only non-writing period of Fanny's entire life. Her resolve to give up writing lasted just nine months after the bonfire before she weakened and began the diary she was to continue for 70 years.

Evelina

Her father's marriage took place in October 1767, thereby adding three Allen stepchildren to the Burney household. Two more Burneys were born of the new marriage, Richard and Sarah Harriet (who also grew up to write novels). The new Mrs Burney was witty and vivacious, but possessed of an evil temper and a disposition to think herself hard-done-by which was not conducive to domestic harmony. Neither her step-children nor her own children could love her, but both families loved Charles, and took care to conceal their differences from him. Being out of the house most of the time he was the happiest subject for a hoodwink.

Between the ages of 15 and 25 Fanny lived quietly at home, keeping out of her step-mother's notice as much as possible, fending off one unwelcome proposal of marriage, often acting as her father's amanuensis by day and carrying on her own writing in her room at night. She wrote her novel *Evelina, or a Young Lady's Entrance into the World* for her own and Susan's amusement, and then copied it out in a feigned hand before her brother Charles, wearing heavy disguise, took it to a publisher. (Fanny was afraid her own handwriting would be recognised from her work in copying her father's manuscripts.) The book was published anonymously in January 1778 and it was only when some months had elapsed bringing favourable notices that Fanny, still half afraid that she had done something he would disapprove of, or which would bring disgrace to the family, showed it to her father.

Not only was he delighted with his daughter's unexpected cleverness, he was far less disposed than she was to preserve her anonymity, seeing the runaway success of the novel as something to bring added lustre to the family name. London society was intrigued as to who might be the author, and Charles had great pleasure in divulging the secret to his friends the Thrales.

Henry Thrale was a rich brewer and Member of Parliament with a town house at Bankside near the brewery and a mansion at Streatham, where his wife Hester Lynch Thrale loved to entertain the intelligentsia of the day, especially Dr Johnson, who was devoted to her. As soon as she found out that the author of the publishing sensation of the year was daughter to her friend Dr Burney, she demanded that Fanny be introduced into their circle.

A warm friendship developed between the two women, despite an 11-year age gap and a great difference in character and demeanour. Fanny was shy, prim, proud (the pride of the socially insecure) and reserved, while Mrs Thrale was emotional, generous, impetuous and demonstrative.[1] For all her wide social circle, however, Mrs Thrale had no really close female friend, and her taciturn, much older husband was no companion to her. Fanny, with her quiet intelligence, good sense and sympathy, came to fill a gap in her life, and Mrs Thrale showed her such true kindness, adapting her approach to suit Fanny's feelings, that the younger woman's fear of being patronised was soothed away. Each enjoyed the other's conversation, for they had literary tastes in common; Mrs Thrale was naturally witty, and Fanny too could talk entertainingly when she was relaxed amongst friends. Fanny began to stay for long periods at Streatham, and at the Thrales' house in Brighton.

[1] Clifford, James L., *Hester Lynch Piozzi (Mrs Thrale)*, OUP, 1968.

Fanny Burney by Edward Francisco Burney, c.1778. *(Reproduced by courtesy of the Brooklyn Museum of Art, New York)*

In 1779 Mr Thrale suffered a stroke, and the following spring he was ordered to Bath for his health. He was to be accompanied by his wife and eldest daughter, the 15-year-old Queeney, and

Fanny was invited to go with them. Her father, pleased with the friendship and with Fanny's new fame and place in society, was all encouragement.

In *Evelina*, Fanny had sent her heroine to spend several weeks at Bristol Hotwells, from where a party drive over to Bath just for one day. These are Evelina's impressions:

> The charming city of Bath answered all my expectations. The Crescent, the prospect from it, and the elegant symmetry of the Circus, delighted me. The Parades, I own, rather disappointed me; one of them is scarce preferable to some of the best paved streets in London, and the other, though it affords a beautiful prospect, a charming view of Prior Park and of the Avon, yet wanted something in itself of more striking elegance than a mere broad pavement, to satisfy the ideas I had formed of it.
>
> At the pump-room, I was amazed at the public exhibition of the ladies in the bath; it is true, their heads were covered with bonnets, but the very idea of being seen, in such a situation, by whoever pleases to look, is indelicate.

Strangely, these are the only two paragraphs describing Bath in all of Fanny Burney's fiction. It is intriguing to consider that Jane Austen, who was unhappy in Bath, chose it as the setting for a large part of two of her novels, while Fanny Burney, who genuinely loved the place, never exploited the intimate knowledge that she was to acquire over the years by using it again in her fiction.

The two paragraphs from *Evelina* could have been written by someone with a very slight acquaintance with the city, which was indeed the case at the time of writing. They seem endearingly to betray the youth of the author in their mixture of horrified modesty and would-be London sophistication. Now, two years after the publication of *Evelina*, Fanny was to get to know the city thoroughly in a three month visit, and to pour out, in letters and journals, her fresh, eager responses to the visual and social experiences it offered.

2. To Bath with Mrs Thrale, 1780

Arrival

'The journey was very comfortable', wrote Fanny to her sister Susan; 'Mr Thrale was charmingly well and in very good spirits, and Mrs Thrale must be charming, well or ill.' They were four days on the road between London and Bath, spending the nights at Maidenhead, Speen Hill and Devizes. In the latter place they were very much impressed with the innkeeper's family, two pretty, musical daughters and 'their brother, a most lovely boy of ten years of age, who seems to be not merely the wonder of their family, but of the times, for his astonishing skill in drawing'. This was the future society portraitist and President of the Royal Academy, Sir Thomas Lawrence.

Writing from Bath on 7th April 1780, Fanny continued:

> I shall now skip to our arrival at this beautiful city, which I really admire more than I did, if possible, when I first saw it. The houses are so elegant, the streets are so beautiful, the prospects so enchanting. I could fill whole pages upon the general beauty of the place and country, but that I have neither time for myself, nor incitements for you, as I know nothing tires so much as description.
>
> We alighted at York House, and Mrs Thrale sent immediately to Sir Philip Jennings Clerke, who spent the Easter holidays here. He came instantly, with his usual alacrity to oblige, and told us of lodgings upon the South Parade, whither in the afternoon we all hied, and Mr Thrale immediately hired a house at the left corner. It was most deliciously situated; we have meadows, hills, Prior Park, 'the soft-flowing Avon' – whatever Nature has to offer, I think, always in our view. My room commands all these; and more luxury for the eye I cannot form a notion of.

The side elevation of 14 South Parade viewed from across the River Avon

Fanny's bedroom must therefore have been on the side elevation, facing across the river. 14 South Parade is of course unusual in being the end house of the terrace, with additional windows let into the side – giving views that are delightfully rural even today. Fanny's would not have been considered the best bedroom, however. Georgian town houses invariably present their principal windows to the street, and the largest bedroom of each house in South Parade, like the drawing room on the first floor and the dining parlour beneath, overlooks the broad handsome pavement which gives the terrace its name.

The front elevation of 14 South Parade

In 1780 it was still a desirable address, though by then nearly 50 years old. The fashionable area of Bath had been moving steadily northwards up the hill towards the Circus and Royal Crescent – the latter just five years old during this first visit of Fanny's – but the Parades had attractions which counteracted their lack of novelty. North and South Parades, with Pierrepont and Duke Streets connecting them, had been laid out in 1738 and built between 1740 and 1748 by the young John Wood as part of a grandiose scheme which got no further but which was intended to mimic Rome with a Royal Forum. It was his second piece of town planning for Bath, the first being Queen Square (in which Fanny was to stay on a subsequent visit). The Parades are in the old low-lying part of the town, so low-lying and close to the river in fact that once it was marshy, but Wood built his houses on great vaults to keep them dry. This also gave him the benefit of raised pavements, one of his purposes being to provide the fashionable visitors to Bath with somewhere dry and spacious to promenade, to see and be seen. That this purpose was still being fulfilled 50 years later, despite the development of other amenities and open places, is evidenced by the Thomas Malton print of 1778 reproduced on the cover of this book. This is just how the scene would have looked to Fanny Burney and the Thrales, as they came and went from their lodgings, just two years later.

Fanny's letter is interesting for its picture of wealthy people arriving in the city for a long visit without knowing where they would be staying. The Thrales slept only one night at the hotel York House before removing to 14 South Parade for three months. This seems to have been the function of hotels, families preferring to take a whole house for the duration of their stay. Only men travelling alone were obliged to put up for long at an hotel, and it was deemed a comfortless kind of arrangement.

Before the development of the Bathwick estate on land beyond Pulteney Bridge in the 1790s, the Parades were among the few locations that were both suitably high in status yet with a level approach to the amenities of the city centre: the Pump-room, the Abbey, the Theatre (then in Orchard Street, not far away) and the Lower Assembly Rooms – not to mention the river walks and Spring Gardens accessible by ferry. Fanny could hardly have had a more comfortable and airy place to stay, and her letter to Susan shows how much she appreciated it.

School of the world

There was an elderly friend of Fanny's father, Samuel Crisp, himself a playwright, who took a particular interest in Fanny's development as a writer. He wrote to her now, 'I am very glad you are now with [the Thrales] in the midst of the Bath circle; your time could not be better employed … You are now at school, the great school of the world, where swarms of new ideas and new characters will continually present themselves before you.' Considering that Fanny came not from a country retreat but from London, that she had known eminent and varied characters at her father's home as well as at Streatham and Brighton with the Thrales, this comment seems a little exaggerated, but it suggests how in 1780 Bath was still considered the best place for a young person to acquire knowledge of the world.

What emerges most strongly from Fanny's account of her three months in Bath is the incessant round of company, the imperative to socialise at every possible hour. This reflected not just the Thrales' own tastes, but the accepted way of life for all fashionable or semi-fashionable visitors to Bath. One day, for example, Fanny was invited out to breakfast and stayed 'prating', as she called it, until twelve o'clock. She then went on to visit another lady and stayed with her 'the rest of the morning'. 'In the afternoon' of the same day, she recorded, 'we all went to the Whalleys' where we found a large and a highly dressed company … We left the Whalleys at nine, and then proceeded to Sir James Caldwell – who had invited us to a concert at his house … We did not get away till late.'

This is perhaps the most extreme example of a day crowded with social engagements, but most mornings saw the ladies making or receiving calls and, following dinner which was more often than not taken *en famille*, they were in company again in the evenings either in their own lodgings or those of their friends. Some of these evenings Fanny found tedious, others enjoyable, depending on the conversational skills of the gathering. 'This evening we spent with old Mrs Cotton and divers other old gentlewomen assembled at her house. Immensely dull work, indeed!' she wrote on one occasion. On the other hand an evening spent in company with the intellectual Mrs Montagu and three other ladies was 'very cheerful and pleasant'. Nevertheless, on the whole, and despite Mr Crisp's high hopes, Fanny decided that 'Bath is as tittle-tattle a town as [King's] Lynn; and people make as many reports, and spread as many idle nothings abroad, as in any little common town in the kingdom'.

Many evening parties were organised round card-playing rather than conversation, but Fanny declined to play, fearing to lose money she could ill afford, for the stakes were often high. Only at home with the Thrales, when she was required to make up a four, did she agree to play.

Though it was much more usual to meet for the evening after dinner, than to be invited for dinner itself, they did occasionally dine out, or have dinner guests themselves – between two and five in number according to Fanny's notes. To be invited after dinner was to be invited 'to drink tea' – the beverage being served an hour or two after the end of dinner, when the gentlemen would rejoin the ladies in the drawing room, and the evening guests would arrive. For example, one day 'Lord Mulgrave and Dr Harrington dined here … In the evening we had more company' (naming seven others). On another occasion they paid an evening visit to Mrs Cholmley, 'who had had company to dinner', ten or eleven people who remained through the evening. There was no sense on the Thrales' part of being offended because they had not been invited to dinner too.

Drinking tea in the evening had quite a ceremony attached to it. The tea was not brought in by the servants, for it was too valuable a commodity to be entrusted to their hands. Rather the beverage would be made and served by one of the females of the household: more often a daughter or other marriageable young lady than the mistress of the house herself. The act of tea-making, from a silver kettle singing on the fire, and of handing round the delicate china cups, prettily displayed not only the hands and arms of the tea-maker, but her obliging manners. Fanny herself was the tea-maker in the Thrale establishment. On one occasion Lord Mulgrave took the opportunity of flirting with her, offering 'If I can be of any use to you here at the Tea Table, out of neighbourly charity, I will'. Fanny 'declined his offer with thanks – but when I was putting away the Tea Chest, "So," he cried, taking it from me, "cannot I put that down? Am I not polished enough for that?" '.

Although by day the Thrales often visited 'the rooms', as Fanny terms them – the two sets of Assembly Rooms in the upper and lower parts of the town – they avoided them by night. Fanny writes of 'showy tonish people who are only to be seen by going to the rooms, which we never do', but whether the Thrales considered themselves less socially elevated or less frivolous than such people is not clear. Only once did they deviate from this rule, when they attended the last ball of the season at the Lower Rooms, but even then Fanny – though asked – would not dance. The evening followed the usual course of Bath balls: minuets followed by country dances, a break for tea, then more country dances. On leaving, 'As we were near home', Fanny wrote, 'we did not get into chairs', suggesting that this was their usual mode of transport in the evenings.

By avoiding the rooms they missed not only balls but concerts, and Fanny, who came from such a musical family, confessed to being 'most greedily hungry for a little music'. This comment was made after a morning visit to hear the playing and singing of a young woman who was subsequently engaged to give lessons to Queeney. The only musical evening she attended was the concert at the private house of Sir James Caldwell already mentioned, and that was a great disappointment. 'How ridiculous to invite so many more people than could be accommodated!' Fanny wrote to Susan, describing the two rooms so crowded that the servants could not get round to serve ice (and the ice was necessary because of the heat and lack of air):

> You may laugh, perhaps, that I have all this time said never a word of the music, but the truth is I scarce heard a note. There were quartettos and overtures by gentlemen performers whose names and faces I knew not, and such was the never-ceasing tattling and noise in the card-room, where I was kept almost all the evening, that a general humming of musical sounds, and now and then a twang, was all I could hear. Nothing could be more ridiculous than a

concert of this sort; and Dr Harrington told me that the confusion amongst the musicians was equal to that among the company; for that, when called upon to open the concert, they found no music.

It seems that the daughters of the house should have provided the music, or otherwise instructed the professionals to bring their own; they did not bring it as a matter of course, as one might expect. Concerts given in private homes often combined performances by amateurs and professionals, as did this one. Dr Harrington's daughter was prevailed upon to play the harpsichord, afterwards complaining that 'she had never touched so vile an instrument', and the daughters of the house sang catches: 'Oh, such singing! worse squalling, more out of tune, and more execrable in every respect, never did I hear.'

One public place certainly not avoided by the Thrales was the theatre, the old theatre in Orchard Street a short distance from their lodgings (not replaced by the present Theatre Royal, higher up the town, until 1806). Fanny mentions going to a play every few evenings – often on their way home from visiting friends, as a spur of the moment decision, it would seem. For example, having had company to dinner at their own lodgings, and then paid an evening visit to friends living at The Belvidere (as Fanny always spelt it; it is one of the terraces lining Lansdown Hill), 'In our way home we stopped at the theatre, and saw the farce of *The Two Misers* – wretched, wretched stuff indeed!'

Fanny was perhaps difficult to please; she was used to London theatres, had seen many plays, and was in the process of writing one of her own; besides which the leading actor of the last few decades, David Garrick, had been a friend of her father and frequenter of their house. But this involvement in the theatre gives weight to her comments. On their very first evening at South Parade:

Mrs Thrale ordered our chairs for the playhouse; Mr Thrale would not accompany us. We were just in time for *The Padlock*, which was almost as bad to me as the company I had just left. Yet the performers here are uncommonly good: some of them as good as almost any we have in town.

Just three days later, 'In the evening we went to the play, and saw *The School for Scandal* and *The Critic*; both of them admirably well acted, and extremely entertaining.' On another occasion:

> At the desire of Miss F Bowdler, we all went to see the play, to see an actress she is dotingly fond of, Mrs Siddons, in *Belvidera*; but instead of falling in love with her, we fell in love with Mr Lee, who played Pierre – and so well! I did not believe such an actor existed now our dear Garrick is gone; a better, except Garrick, never did I see – nor any one nearly equal to him – for sense, animation, looks, voice, grace – Oh, for everything the part would admit – he is indeed delightful.

She saw him again later in Shakespeare: 'We went to see *The Merchant of Venice* … My favourite Mr Lee played Shylock, and played it incomparably. With the rest of the performers I was not too much charmed'. She was equally delighted with him in the part of Norval in the popular play *Douglas* by John Home. The Miss Bowdler referred to, incidentally, a frequent associate of Fanny's in Bath, was sister to that Thomas Bowdler whose surname has passed into the English language through his mauling of Shakespeare.

People and places

What really called forth Fanny's enthusiasm was walking and admiring the scenery, natural and man-made. During the week of their arrival:

> Tuesday morning we spent in walking all over the town, viewing the beautiful Circus, the company-crowded Pump-room, and the demi-divine Crescent, which, to all the excellence of architecture that adorns the Circus, adds all the delights of nature that beautify the Parades.

On another occasion 'We walked in the beautiful meadows round the city all the morning'. There is a reference to 'sauntering on the Parade with Mr Thrale', and by May the weather was so warm that Mrs Thrale could write, 'Our flagstones upon the South Parade burn one's feet through one's shoes; but the Bath belles, fearless of fire ordeal, trip about, secure in cork soles'.[1] But Mr Thrale was not allowed to get away with only sauntering. Unable or unwilling to curb his overeating, and his health giving cause for alarm, he had been advised to take as much exercise as possible. So, Fanny wrote, 'I went to the Belvidere, and made Mr Thrale accompany me by way of exercise, for the Belvidere is near a mile from our house, and all up hill'. (Mr Thrale's overeating was a serious problem. As his wife wrote to Dr Johnson at this time, 'He looks well enough, but I have no notion of health for a man whose mouth cannot be sewed up. Burney and I and Queeney tease him every meal he eats, and Mrs Montagu is quite serious with him, but what *can* one do? He will eat, I think, and if he does eat I know he will not live; it makes me very unhappy, but I must bear it.'[2])

The Belvidere was a regular destination for their walks, since they had acquaintances living there. 'The Belvidere is a most beautiful spot', Fanny wrote; 'it is on a high hill, at one of the extremities of the town, of which, as of the Avon and all the adjacent country, it commands a view that is quite enchanting'.

She describes two visits to the Spring Gardens, pleasure grounds laid out on the opposite side of the Avon from South Parade. Once they met by appointment a party of friends at the Pump-room, and proceeded to Spring Gardens (which were reached by ferry) for a public breakfast. The other visit was very much more impromptu. Their dinner guest one day, the Bishop of Peterborough, 'who was in very high spirits, proposed a frolic, which was, that we should all go to Spring Gardens, where he should give us tea, and thence proceed to Mr Ferry's, to see a very curious house and garden'. Mrs Thrale protested that she had invited company to tea, but the Bishop promised they should be back in good time and 'was so gaily authoritative that he gained his point'. Accordingly:

[1] This and all other quotations from Mrs Thrale's diaries are taken from *Thraliana*, 2 volumes, edited by Katherine C Balderston, OUP, 1951.
[2] Quoted in Seeley, L.B., *Mrs Thrale*, Seeley & Co., 1890.

The three Thrales, the bishop and I pursued our scheme, crossed the Avon, had a sweet walk through the meadows, and drank tea at Spring Gardens, where the bishop did the honours with a spirit, a gaiety, and an activity that jovialised us all, and really we were prodigiously lively. We then walked on to Mr Ferry's habitation.

Mr Ferry is a Bath alderman; his house and garden exhibit the house and garden of Mr Tattersall, enlarged. Just the same taste prevails, the same paltry ornaments, the same crowd of buildings, the same unmeaning decoration, and the same unsuccessful attempts at making something of nothing.

They kept us half an hour in the garden, while they were preparing for our reception in the house, where after parading through four or five little vulgarly showy closets, not rooms, we were conducted into a very gaudy little apartment, where the master of the house sat reclining on his arm, as if in contemplation, though everything conspired to show that the house and its inhabitants were carefully arranged for our reception. The bishop had sent in his name by way of gaining admission.

The bishop, with a gravity of demeanour difficult to himself to sustain, apologised for our intrusion, and returned thanks for seeing the house and garden. Mr Ferry started from his pensive attitude, and begged us to be seated, and then a curtain was drawn, and we perceived through a glass a perspective view of ships, boats and water! This raree-show over, the maid who officiated as show-woman had a hint given her, and presently a trap-door opened, and up jumped a covered table, ornamented with various devices. When we had expressed our delight at this long enough to satisfy Mr Ferry, another hint was given, and presently down dropped an eagle from the ceiling, whose talons were put into a certain hook at the top of the covering of the table, and when the admiration at

this was over, up again flew the eagle, conveying
in his talons the cover, and leaving under it a repast
of cakes, sweetmeats, oranges and jellies.

With all this and more to detain them, and to laugh about as
they walked home, it was only when they were crossing the river
again that they realised quite how much time had elapsed, by the
sight of the South Parade windows full of the company who had
come to tea – leaving Mrs Thrale 'in horrid confusion' at the breach
of etiquette into which she had been betrayed. The curious house
was Bathwick Villa, home of Alderman Ferry, the City Chamberlain,
dismissed in this very year of 1780 owing to his failure to balance
the books of the City Treasury. Three years later Bathwick Villa was
to be sold to Mr Marett, a wine merchant, and opened to the general
public; for an annual subscription of 2s.6d (12^{1}/$_{2}$p) he provided tea
gardens, newspapers, dinners, suppers and fireworks. A ferry to
Bathwick Villa operated near the site of the present Cleveland Bridge.

Another singular habitation of an eccentric owner visited by
Fanny was the villa at Batheaston – a few miles east of Bath – home
of Lady Miller. Here, in a bow window overlooking the Avon, was
kept a Frascati vase into which, on certain Thursdays of the year,
guests were invited to drop poetical contributions – which were
eventually published in four volumes. 'Notwithstanding Batheaston
is so much laughed at in London', wrote Fanny, 'nothing here is
more tonish than to visit Lady Miller, who is extremely curious in
her company, admitting few people who are not of rank or of fame,
and excluding of those all who are not people of character very
unblemished.' Naturally, Fanny and the Thrales passed this test
and were invited to the villa, which held its usual Thursday
complement of company, though 'the business of the vase is over
for this season' and Fanny only saw 'the place appropriated for the
vase', not the vase itself. Lady Miller herself Fanny described as:

a round, plump, coarse-looking dame of about
forty, and while all her aim is to appear an elegant
woman of fashion, all her success is to seem an
ordinary woman in very common life, with fine
clothes on. Her manners are bustling, her air mock-
important, and her manners very inelegant.

Joshua Reynolds (1723-1792), Mrs Thrale and her Daughter Hester (Queeney), 1781, oil on canvas, 148.6 x 140.3 cm. *(Gift of Lord Beaverbrook, The Beaverbrook Art Gallery, Fredericton, New Brunswick, Canada)*

However, Fanny added, she seemed extremely good-natured and civil.

An introduction which Fanny narrowly avoided, to her great relief, was to a relation of her godmother, Mrs Greville: Mrs Macartney, a resident of Bath who liked to be known as the Queen of Bath. Fanny was told she was 'one of the worst women breathing; a drunkard notoriously, an assistant to the vices of others, & an infamous practitioner of all species of them herself'. By keeping a good house and laying on extravagant enter-tainments, Mrs Macartney 'contrived to get company to her mansion & be countenanced by people of character and rank'. Mrs Thrale, always game for new acquaintance, accepted an invitation for herself, Fanny and Queeney, but managed to wriggle out of it when the horrified Fanny enlightened her as to the lady's reputation. However, Fanny enjoyed ogling her from a distance at the Lower Rooms. Her face, wrote Fanny,

> is bold, hardened, painted, snuff, leering & impudent! Her dress, too, was of the same cast, a thin muslin short sacque & coat lined throughout with pink … & a something of a very short cloak half concealed about half of her old wrinkled neck – the rest was visible to disgust the beholders – red bows and ribbons in abundance, a gauze bonnet tipped onto the top of her head, & a pair of mittens!
>
> … The dreadful character I had heard of this woman made me shrink from the very notion of visiting her, nor could I bear that one of Mrs Thrale's fame & celebrity & purity of mind & conduct should countenance a wretch notorious for all manner of evil; a wretch who, Miss Bowdler has told me, endeavours as much, by dispersing obscene books, to corrupt youth, as to assist already corrupted maturity in the prosecution of vice!'

Excusing herself to a correspondent for long gaps between letters (though the length of the letters she did write during this Bath visit makes one marvel how she fitted them into such busy days and evenings), Fanny writes of her time being taken up with 'engagements, dress and work'. By the latter she meant not novel-writing, or any kind of writing, but needlework. That dress was time-consuming was not because of any inordinate interest of Fanny's in the subject, but rather the reverse, so that achieving the right, elaborate appearance was a chore to her. She never records any of her own outfits, and one popular Bath pastime for females that the diaries are silent about is shopping. However, a glimpse into the buying habits of the wealthy is given when she tells Susan of an episode that reflects well on the Thrales:

The kindness of this family seems daily to increase upon me; not indeed that of Mrs Thrale, for it cannot, so sweetly and delightfully she keeps it up; she has not left herself power to do more; – but Mr Thrale evidently interests himself more and more about me weekly – as does his fair daughter.

This morning a milliner was ordered to bring whatever she had to recommend, I believe, to our habitation, and Mr Thrale bid his wife and daughter take what they wanted, and send him the account.

But, not content with this, he charged me to do the same. You may imagine if I did. However, finding me refractory, he absolutely insisted upon presenting me with a complete suit of gauze lino, and that in a manner that showed me a refusal would greatly disoblige him. And then he very gravely desired me to have whatever I pleased at any time, and to have it added to his account. And so sincere I knew him to be, that I am sure he would be rather pleased than surprised if I should run him up a new bill at this woman's. He would fain have persuaded me to have taken abundance of other things, and Mrs Thrale seemed more gratified than with what he did for herself.

And on another occasion, 'Mr Thrale would fain have presented me with a very pretty gown, when he bought one for his wife and daughter, but I would not take it!'

On Sundays the Thrales and Fanny invariably attended church. They began by patronising St James's. On their first Sunday in Bath they 'heard a very indifferent preacher' there, and 'returned to read better sermons of our own choosing' (in many ways, Fanny seems to have been a Victorian before her time). The sermons she most admired were both preached by visiting bishops. One diary entry reads:

Sunday.– This morning Miss Gregory came to accompany us to St James's Church, to hear Dr Porteus, Bishop of Chester, preach a charity sermon for an excellent institution here, to enable the poor sick to drink the waters in an hospital. It was an admirable sermon, rational, judicious, forcible, and truth-breathing; and delivered with a clearness, stillness, grace, and propriety that softened and bettered us all – as, I believe, appeared in the collection, for I fancy not a soul left the church without offering a mite.

The other bishop was the one who enticed them to Spring Gardens, the Bishop of Peterborough, John Hinchcliffe. Describing him as 'a most shining and superior man – gay, high-spirited, manly, quick and penetrating', Fanny wrote that 'he adores, and is adored in return by Mrs Thrale'. (He was just nine years her senior; Mrs Thrale herself recorded in her diary that at Bath he 'treated me with public teadrinkings & a long et cetera of friendship and flirtation'.) For him they forsook St James's. 'We went to the abbey, to hear the bishop preach. He gave us a very excellent sermon, upon the right use of seeking knowledge, namely, to know our Creator by his works, and to learn our own duty by studying his power.'

The following Sunday they were at the Abbey again, to hear 'an excellent sermon from the Bishop of Peterborough, who preached merely at the request of Mrs Thrale'! Having by now changed their habits, the next week they again worshipped in the Abbey – Fanny does not mention who the preacher was – and afterwards she spent an hour or two looking over the Abbey and reading the memorials, including one erected by a Dr Hoadley to the novelist Sarah Fielding. 'Will any future doctor do as much for me?' mused Fanny.

The Blue Stockings

Two of the literary ladies known collectively as the Blue Stockings were in Bath during Fanny's visit. Friends of Dr Johnson, some of them contributors to his magazine *The Rambler*, they obtained their nickname not from their own apparel but from the daytime stockings of blue worsted worn to their evening receptions by one of their male admirers, too poor to afford correct evening dress. They were a generation older than Fanny; of the two whom Fanny met in Bath, Elizabeth Carter had been born in 1717 and Elizabeth Montagu in 1720. The latter had lodgings in The Circus. Learned and sociable, they were renowned not only for their writing but for the quality of their conversation. Indeed their salons, frequented by both men and women, had been established in the 1750s expressly to promote rational conversation as an alternative to gambling by way of evening entertainment.

Their strange nickname was used affectionately by some, derisively by others. Fanny's own name for them was The Witlings, and she wrote a play with this name at about this time, which her father, who was always nervous about offending the great and the good, eventually persuaded her to withdraw. Not that Fanny wished only to mock; she had genuine admiration for these women. 'We see Mrs Montagu very often, and I have already spent six evenings with her at various houses', she wrote when they had been in Bath about three weeks:

> I am very glad at this opportunity of seeing so much of her; for, allowing a little for parade and ostentation, which her power in wealth, and rank in literature, offer some excuse for, her conversation is very agreeable; she is always reasonable and sensible, and sometimes instructive and entertaining; and I think of our Mrs Thrale, we say the reverse, for she is always entertaining and instructive, and sometimes reasonable and sensible; and I write this because she is just now looking over me – not but what I think it too!

Mrs Thrale's own sense of the rivalry between them appears in her summing up, at the end of the visit: 'Mrs Montagu & I liveda vast deal together at Bath this Spring; we met & were *pitted* every night at one house or another; it came to that at last, that I observed to Fanny Burney, we might now say quite fairly, "Satan! I know thy strength, and thou know'st mine".' Bath evenings in 1780 were evidently serious affairs – for those that took themselves seriously, at least.

Elizabeth Montagu, engraving, artist unknown. *(Reproduced by courtesy of the Trustees of the Johnson House Museum, London)*

Fanny also met Mrs Carter, though more briefly. She was in Bath for just one day, and was of the company invited to tea at 14 South Parade on the occasion when they were late home after the jaunt to Spring Gardens with the Bishop. Mrs Carter had been waiting for them an hour. Fanny depicts the scene:

As soon as the general apologies were over, Miss Cooper, who knew my earnest desire of being introduced to Mrs Carter, kindly came up to me, and taking my hand, led me to her venerable friend, and told her who I was. Mrs Carter arose, and received me with a smiling air of benevolence that more than answered all my expectations of her. She is really a noble-looking woman; I never saw age so graceful in the female sex yet; her whole face seems to beam with goodness, piety, and philanthropy.

She told me she had lately seen some relations of mine at Mrs Ord's who had greatly delighted her by their musical talents – meaning, I found, Mr Burney and our Etty; and she said something further in their praise, and of the pleasure they had given her; but as I was standing in a large circle, all looking on, and as I kept her standing, I could hardly understand what she said, and soon after returned to my seat.

She scarce stayed three minutes longer. When she had left the room, I could not forbear following her to the head of the stairs, on the pretence of inquiring for her cloak. She then turned round to me, and looking at me with an air of much kindness, said, 'Miss Burney, I have been greatly obliged to you long before I have seen you, and must now thank you for the very great entertainment you have given me.'

This was so unexpected a compliment that I was too much astonished to make any answer. However, I am very proud of it from Mrs Carter, and I will not fail to seek another meeting with her when I return to town – which I shall be able to do by means of Miss Cooper, or Miss Ord, or Mrs Pepys.

The literary figure whom Fanny Burney found most disappointing was Christopher Anstey, author of the satiric rhyming *New Bath Guide*, published in 1766 and hugely popular (as is often the case) with the very people whose habits and excesses he was poking fun at. Fanny Burney called it 'so excellent, so diverting, so original a satire' and has her hero and heroine Lord Orville and Evelina read it together not so much for fun as for moral instruction. She was therefore looking forward to seeing and listening to the conversation of this admired writer on his home ground. Bath was not only Anstey's subject but his place of residence; from 1770 to his death in 1805 he occupied 5 Royal Crescent.

'I heard but little that he said, and that little was scarce worth hearing', wrote Fanny after being in company with him for the first time. 'He had no opportunity of shining, and was as much like another man as you can imagine. It is very unfair to expect wonders from a man all at once; yet it was impossible to help being disappointed, because his air, look and manner are mighty heavy and unfavourable to him.' On a second meeting she was ambivalent: 'Mr Anstey opens rather more, and approaches nearer being agreeable. If he could but forget he had written the *Bath Guide*, with how much more pleasure would everybody else remember it.' By a third meeting she had settled her views, and they were not in his favour; he was, she decided, in a well-turned phrase, 'shyly important, and silently proud'.

Fanny might have stopped to reflect that she herself was extremely shy, inclined to be silent when among strangers, and that her pride was called forth at the slightest hint of patronage or flattery. She too might have been a disappointment to the public who had enjoyed her novel and now expected her conversation to sparkle like the lines of her dialogue. She would not shine to order. Her Bath journal reveals her distaste for being noticed and her habit of rebuffing those who, whether sincerely or sycophantically, showered praises on her. No small number of the people she met in Bath were thrilled to find they were in company with the author of the best-selling novel of the last two years, and she had to endure an 'abundance of civil speeches about *Evelina'*, a sample of which she reproduced verbatim for Susan:

> 'Oh, miss, you deserve everything! You've writ the best and prettiest book. That lord there – I forget his name, that marries her at last – what a fine gentleman he is! You deserve everything for drawing such a character; and then Miss Elena, there, Miss Belmont, as she is at last – what a noble couple of 'em you have put together! As to t'other lord, I was glad he had not her, for I see he had nothing but a bad design.'

Another young lady told Miss Thrale, 'I am going to the library immediately for the book; though I assure you I read it all when it first came out; but that was nothing like, not knowing anything of the matter; but Mrs Dobson has let me into the secret [of Fanny's authorship]'. Nor was it only the female response which could be tiresome. As Mrs Thrale somewhat impatiently summed up on looking back over the visit:

> Miss Burney was much admired at Bath, the puppy men said she had such a drooping air, & such a timid intelligence; or a timid air I think it was and a drooping intelligence; never sure was such a collection of pedantry & affectation as filled Bath when we were on that spot.

The Gordon Riots

Such concerns were put aside, however, in the events which overwhelmed them when they had been in Bath three months. Bath was suddenly, and terrifyingly, caught up in what are known to history as the Gordon Riots. Their origin lay in the Roman Catholic Relief Bill of 1778, which had restored most civil rights to Catholics, and which, since Popery seemed no longer a threat to the country, had passed easily through both Houses of Parliament. But among some of the rougher elements of London society there was some remaining bigotry – or maybe just grievances of an unfocused nature, ripe for some demagogue to channel. Such a man was the unbalanced Lord George Gordon, who in early June 1780 led 60,000 rabble in a march on the Commons demanding the repeal of the Act.

Various acts of lawlessness followed over the next several days, mainly looting, arson and prison-breaking. Catholic chapels and the homes of known or supposed Catholics were the chief targets, though much of the violence was indiscriminate. The whole episode lasted a week, from 2nd to 9th June, by which time troops had regained control and Lord George Gordon had been clapped in the Tower.

As far as the history books are concerned, the trouble was confined to London. The journal of Fanny Burney proves otherwise. On Friday 9th June, when the rioting in London was effectively over, Fanny wrote:

> Friday – on our return home we were informed a mob was surrounding the new Roman Catholic chapel. At first we disbelieved it, but presently one of the servants came and told us they were knocking it to pieces; and in half an hour, looking out of the windows, we saw it in flames! And listening, we heard loud and violent shouts! Mrs Thrale and I sat up till four o'clock, and walked about the Parades, and at two we went with a large party to the spot, and saw the beautiful new building consuming; the mob were then all quiet – all still and silent, and everybody seemed but as spectators.

'Alas! to what have we all lived! – the poor invalids here will probably lose all chance of life from terror', Fanny wrote. 'The Catholics throughout the place are all threatened with destruction, and we met several porters, between ten and eleven at night, privately removing goods, walking on tiptoe, and scarcely breathing.'

The next morning's post brought letters informing the Thrales that their town house at Bankside and mansion at Streatham had both been attacked. In that day's Bath and Bristol newspaper Mr Thrale, who had voted for the Bill in the Commons, was asserted to be a papist: 'a villainous falsehood' in Fanny's words. Terrified for his safety if they remained in Bath, they 'settled to decamp', but it took them most of Saturday to pack and arrange their affairs. They had originally intended to go on to Bristol when they left Bath, but that now appeared madness, for they were told there were seven 'Romish' chapels there. Instead they would travel about the country, stopping only in the quietest places, and hope to get safely to their Brighton retreat. 'Tonight we shall stop at Warminster', wrote Fanny, 'not daring to go to Devizes'.

Meanwhile she noted that all the stage coaches coming in from London were chalked 'No Popery', as were walls and doors in Bath itself. As they left Bath at eight o'clock in the evening, their anxiety not to remain another night outweighing the dangers and discomfort of travelling in the dark, the city was filled with 'dragoons, militia, and armed constables, not armed with muskets, but bludgeons'. Bath's chairmen, known for their strength, perhaps, had been sworn in by the mayor that morning for petty constables – a detail that brings her world close to that of Shakespeare. Travelling by coach-and-four, with two men on horseback, the Thrales reached Warminster a little before midnight, and went on to Salisbury the next day. Both places were perfectly peaceful, and at Salisbury they heard the good news that Lord George Gordon was in the Tower, and it was safe to return to London and their respective families.

So ended an eventful visit to Bath. At the height of their alarm, Mrs Thrale had sat down to write to Dr Johnson, dating her letter 'Bath, 3 o'clock on Saturday morning, June 10 1780'. (He had often admonished her for not dating her letters very fully.)

> Oh, my dear Sir! was I ever particular in dating a letter before? And is this a time to begin to be particular, when I have been up all night in trembling agitation, and only write now to drive time forward till the post comes in? … Miss Burney

is frighted; but she says better times will come. She made me date my letter so, and persists in hoping that ten years hence we shall all three read it over together, and be merry. Oh, no, no, no! Here is a poor prospect of merriment. The flames of the Romish chapel are not yet extinguished, and the rioters are going to Bristol to burn that. Their shouts are still in my ears; and I do not believe a dog or cat in the town sleeps this night. Mr Thrale seems thunder-stricken, he don't mind anything; and Queeney's curiosity is stronger than her fears ...[1]

To which Dr Johnson replied: 'I received your letter of battle and conflagration. You certainly do right in retiring; for who can guess the caprice of the rabble? My master and Queeney are dear people for not being frighted, and you and Burney are dear people for being frighted ...'.[2] His affection for them all is touching. But though Fanny was correct in looking forward to calmer times on the streets, she was wrong in her prediction that ten years hence they would 'all three' read Mrs Thrale's letter together 'and be merry'. By 1790, Dr Johnson had been dead six years, and the two women, once so close, had become totally estranged from each other.

[1] Quoted in Seeley, L.B., *Mrs Thrale*, Seeley & Co., 1890.
[2] *ibid.*

3. Bath Revisited, 1791

An invitation declined

The 1780s were an unhappy decade for Fanny Burney. Persuaded to abandon her play, she was urged by her father to write another novel quickly, while *Evelina* was still in the public consciousness. The result was the publication in 1782 of *Cecilia, or Memoirs of an Heiress*, the copyright of which Charles sold on her behalf for £250, which turned out to be a bad bargain. Its composition had not been as pleasurable to her as that of *Evelina*, in fact it cost her both physical and mental exhaustion, but it was eagerly awaited by the public and sold well.

She was in need of a holiday, and in April 1983 she was again invited to accompany Mrs Thrale to Bath. This time her father advised her not to go – indeed, virtually forbade her to go. Circumstances were very different from what they had been three years earlier, for Mrs Thrale was now a widow and behaving, in the eyes of much of the world, with shocking impropriety.

In April 1781, after eating yet another huge meal, Henry Thrale had collapsed and died. Though racing to finish her novel, Fanny supported her friend through the initial shock and grief, and the complications of sorting out his affairs and how the brewery should be managed. But the cause of the eventual rift between Fanny Burney and Hester Thrale was already on the horizon. Gabriel Piozzi, an Italian singer and music teacher some six months older than Mrs Thrale (they were both 40 at the time of Mr Thrale's death), had been introduced to her in the London home of Dr Burney in 1778. At the time she had taken little notice of him. But happening to meet him again in Brighton shortly after the Gordon Riots episode, she prevailed on him to come to Streatham and give music lessons to Queeney. By the summer after her husband's death, it was becoming apparent that Mrs Thrale was romantically interested in the Italian. She behaved as circumspectly as she could, given her impetuous and open personality, but she had never been in love before (her marriage having been an arranged one) and her passion gradually became evident to those around her. Everybody opposed the match, most especially her daughters and their legal guardians, fearing that the social degradation would hamper their own chances of advantageous marriages. Dr Johnson was horrified, Dr Burney was horrified, everybody was horrified. Fanny continued to give her friend a sympathetic ear and wise counsel (as she saw it), but like everybody else she could only regard the attraction as a disaster, and Mrs Thrale's giving way to it as unseemly. 'Children, religion, friends, country and character', enumerated Fanny in a letter designed to fortify her friend's mind, 'All is at stake, – & for what? – a gratification that no man can *esteem*, not even he for whom you feel it.'

1782 was a year of emotional turmoil for them both, as the older woman was torn between what she saw as her right to happiness, and what was represented to her, by all her friends, as her duty. In January 1783 Fanny told her that she must either marry Gabriel Piozzi immediately or renounce him forever, otherwise her reputation would be irretrievably lost. On the 27th of that month, which was her 42nd birthday, Mrs Thrale broken-heartedly sent Piozzi away. He prepared to return to Italy, and she made plans to live quietly and economically in Bath ('if possible on £1000 per annum, that I may save money enough to pay my debts, and fly to the man of my heart', she confided in her diary). She would have appreciated Fanny's companionship and support in Bath, but though often longing to go, Fanny would not do so against her father's wishes. For almost a year Mrs Thrale kept a room aired and ready for Fanny in her house in Russell Street, and wrote to her almost daily, letters that continued to be full of anguish and frustrated love.

Charles Burney was right in thinking that though Piozzi was banished, Mrs Thrale had not given up hopes of marrying him. By the end of the year Queeney Thrale, always the most implacable, and apparently the most heartless, of opponents to the match, had become convinced that her mother might actually die if the separation continued. With Queeney's consent, therefore, he was recalled. That was in December 1783. It was the beginning of June 1784 before Piozzi actually set out on the journey back to England. He arrived towards the end of the month, and after waiting the legal 26 days, was married to Mrs Thrale in a Roman Catholic ceremony in London, to be followed by a Protestant one at St James's church, Bath. In September they set off for a long (two and a half years) tour of Italy, leaving the four Miss Thrales, ranging in age from seven to twenty, under the care of their legal guardians.

For some time Mrs Thrale had suspected that her friend Fanny Burney was siding too much with Queeney, going behind her back to bolster her daughter's implacability. The truth is that Fanny did oppose the marriage, but she had never made any pretence otherwise, and she certainly advised Queeney's capitulation rather than see her mother suffer a total breakdown of health. When the marriage eventually took place, the formal letter of congratulation that Fanny sent Mrs Piozzi offended her deeply by not including the bridegroom in her wishes for future happiness. More brief letters were exchanged, but they only served to offend further, and to the last of Fanny's letters Mrs Piozzi made no reply.

Dr Johnson, too, had hurt Mrs Piozzi by writing to her that she was 'ignominiously married', but he had the grace to retract. Their old footing of intimacy could never have been recovered, however, even had there been more time. Within three months of her departure for Italy, Dr Johnson was dead of a stroke, having told Fanny during their last meeting that his friend of 20 years had 'disgraced herself, disgraced her friends & connections, disgraced her sex, & disgraced all the expectations of mankind'.

These were not Fanny's only griefs in the 1780s. For two or three years in the early part of the decade she entertained hopes of a proposal of marriage from a clergyman, George Owen Cambridge, whose attentions to her appeared to mean something, and with whom, since he seemed an honourable and intelligent man, she felt she could be happy. But no proposal came, not even when she made sure he was aware of the action she was about to take. In the summer of 1786 she allowed herself to be bullied by her father into accepting an appointment at Court as Second Keeper of the Queen's Robes to Queen Charlotte, wife of George III. The position and her duties were wholly

Fanny Burney, engraving after the portrait by Edward Francisco Burney, 1782. *(Reproduced by courtesy of the Trustees of the Johnson House Museum)*

uncongenial to her, although she did become personally fond of both the Queen and the King (whose first bout of madness she was to observe at close quarters; her diary contains a vivid account of his chasing her round the shrubbery at Kew). Five stultifying years in Court, without a single holiday, coming on top of her other sorrows, almost broke her in spirits and health. With a footman and maid of her own, a stipend of £200 per annum, and of course her bed and board, her father had intended this to be her honourable provision for life, but after five years she and her sisters had to beg him to consent to her petitioning the Queen for her release. He gave in, but remained puzzled why she had not been happy at Court, and worried that their Majesties would be offended at her wish for release.

To take the waters

Fanny left the Court in July 1791. She was 39 years old, exhausted and ill. The bloom of youth and health and hope had gone. It was nine years since she had written a novel, 16 years since she had received a proposal of marriage. The Streatham circle, which had been her second home, her source of intellectual friendship, was broken up. The future seemed empty and hopeless.

All her sisters were married with domestic responsibilities, but a kind friend, Mrs Ord, offered to accompany her on a convalescent tour of the West Country. A staunch Tory (which was to have some significance as it happened on this visit), Anna Ord was a widow, 26 years older than Fanny. Setting off on 1st August, they travelled in Mrs Ord's coach and four, covering roughly 30 miles a day, through Hampshire, Wiltshire and Dorset before pausing at Sidmouth, Devon, for a week. Then via Exeter and Taunton to Wells, where there was a sudden change of plan. They had always intended to close the tour with a fortnight at Bristol – Fanny had actually requested her father to send a letter to be picked up at the post office there – but 'at night, upon a deeply deliberate investigation in the medical way, – it was suddenly resolved that we should proceed to Bath, instead of Bristol, & that I should try there first the stream of King Bladud'. On Saturday 20th August 1791, therefore, the two ladies arrived in Bath, taking lodgings in Queen Square.

It was 11 years since Fanny had seen the city, and she was amazed by its growth during that time, as well she might. Her visit occurred in the middle of Bath's building boom, which lasted from 1788 to 1793. Between 1780, when Fanny had known the city so well, and 1793, when a spectacular financial crash brought the boom to an end, the number of houses in Bath increased by a massive 45 percent. Most of these were built in the five years of the boom, so that Fanny saw them either as very new houses or as building sites. An easy and abundant supply of credit following the end of the war with America meant that, according to a recent economic historian of Bath, 'the boom was characterised as much by a financial as by a building mania, and that it was generated more from the supply than the demand side'.[1] Nonetheless demand was surely there, as more and more people found it within their means to travel and take holidays. On the perimeter of the city, much speculative building was taking place, especially along the London Road and on the higher reaches of Lansdown Hill – Camden and Lansdown Crescents, with their attendant streets. The Bathwick meadows were also being built on, with Laura Place recently finished and the magnificent Great Pulteney Street actually in the process of building when Fanny visited. She wrote to Susan:

> Bath is extremely altered since I last visited it. Its circumference is perhaps trebled: but its buildings are so unfinished, so spread, so every where beginning, & no where ending, that it looks rather like a space of Ground lately fixed upon for creating a Town, than a Town itself, of many years duration.
>
> It is beautiful and wonderful throughout. The hills are built up & down, & the vales so stocked with streets and houses, that, in some places, from the ground floor on one side a street, you cross over to the attic of your opposite neighbour. The white stone, where clean, has a beautiful effect, & even where worn, a grand one. But I must not write a literal Bath Guide – & a figurative one Anstey has all to himself. I will only tell you, in brief, yet in truth – it looks a city of palaces – a town of hills, & a hill of towns.

[1] Neale, R.S., *Bath 1680-1850, A Social History*, Routledge & Kegan Paul, 1981.

The City Corporation too was caught up in speculation fever. In March 1788, the same month that the first stone was laid in Laura Place, the Corporation voted to proceed with a plan to improve the area round the baths and provide better access from the upper part of the town. The Pump-room was rebuilt and the area around it opened up. A new street called Bath Street was created to take bathers from the Pump-room to the newly built Cross Bath. With a colonnaded pavement on both sides, enabling pedestrians to move between the two establishments in the dry, and opening out at either end into a segmented curve, Bath Street brought much elegance right to the heart of the baths area, which had formerly been confined within the medieval street plan.

While the outlying areas could be avoided by the public until they were ready for habitation, the redevelopment of the centre of the city was bound to cause some temporary discomfort to visitors, as Fanny described in a letter to another sister, Hetty:

> This city is so filled with workmen, dust & lime, that you really want two pair of eyes to walk about in it – one for being put out, & the other to see with afterwards. But as I, however, have only one pair, which are pretty much dedicated to the first purpose, you cannot, in reason, expect from me a very distinct description of it. Bath seems, now, rather a collection of small towns, or of magnificent villas, than one city. They are now building as if the world was just beginning, & this was the only spot on which its inhabitants could endure to reside. Nothing is secure from their architectural rage. They build upon the pinnacle of hills that only to look up to breaks one's neck – & they build in the deepest depths below, which only to look down upon makes one giddy. Even the streets round the Pump-room are pulling down for new edifices, & you can only drink from their choice stream, by wading through their chosen mud. Their plans seem all to be formed without the least reference to what adjoins or surrounds them, they are therefore high, low, broad, narrow, long, short, in manners

the most unexpected, & by interruptions the most abrupt: – & some of their houses are placed so zig-zag, in & out, you would suppose them built first, & then dropt, to find their own foundations. They seem seldom to attempt levelling the ground for the sake of uniformity, but, very contentedly, when they have raised one house on the spot where it could stand most conveniently, they raise the next upon its nearest & steepest aclivity, so precisely above it, that from the garret of one, you *mount* into the kitchen of the other. One street, leading out of Laura Place, of a noble width, & with broad handsome pavement, pompously labelled at the corner JOHNSON STREET, has in it – only one house: – nor can another be added, for it opens to Spring Gardens, & even its vis-à-vis is occupied by the dead wall belonging to a house in Laura Place. Nor can you make a visit from one street to another, without such an ascent, or such a declivity, that you must have the wheel of the carriage *locked* to go from neighbour to neighbour. – You will ask me if I mean to set you up with materials for making a model of Bath? but I am perfectly content with having given you a model of confusion.

Certainly, unless you are advised to come hither for health, I should advise you not to see this place these two years, at least, for pleasure; as the avenues to the Pump rooms will not sooner be finished, & walking here in winter must be next to impracticable. However, when all these works are completed, & the completers, with the usual gratitude of the world, are driven aloof, this city, already the most splendid of England, will be as noble as can be conceived.

Fanny showed remarkable prescience in this last comment. Thomas Baldwin, appointed Deputy Chamberlain and Surveyor in 1785, was in charge of the redevelopment of the baths area for the Corporation at an annual salary of £210, as well as being the chief developer, on his own account, of the Bathwick estate for the Pulteney family who owned the land. With too much to oversee, he got into difficulties with his book-keeping, and when the Napoleonic wars caused a general recession in 1793, Baldwin was one of those who went bankrupt. He lost his position and his property and was to die in 1820 hardly noticed, though he had done more than any architect but the Woods to create Georgian Bath.

Fanny was alive not only to the material changes to Bath but to the human ones. 'O how have I thought', she wrote to Susan, 'in patroling it – of my poor Mrs Thrale! – I went to look, & sigh at the sight, at the house on North Parade where we dwelt [a slip for South Parade] – & almost every old place brings to my mind some scene in which we were engaged.' Not only the Thrales, but most of the families she had known 11 years ago had 'altered & dispersed', with many deaths among them.

As a friend and companion, Mrs Ord was no substitute for Mrs Thrale. On the one hand, Fanny acknowledged, 'It is impossible to tell you how kind, good & considerate is our excellent Mrs Ord'; but six weeks of being always together necessarily revealed the faults of each to the other, and Fanny described Mrs Ord's: 'She thinks the worst, & judges the most severely of all mankind, of any person I have ever known. It is the standing imperfection of her character, & so ungenial, so nipping, so blighting, it sometimes damps all my pleasure in her society, since my living with her has shown the extent of her want of all charity towards her fellows.' This judgement came about principally because of a disagreement between the two ladies about some grand acquaintance in Bath.

The Spencers

In her present state of poor spirits and feeble health, Fanny believed she had no wish to make new acquaintance, or to socialise to anything like the same extent as in 1780. Mrs Ord, who was content just to see a few old friends of her own, respected her wishes; and the times too were favourable for Fanny. With the huge increase in the resident and visiting population of Bath came a decrease in communal life. It was no longer the case that 'everybody who was anybody' sought each other out in the evenings as a matter of course. There were simply too many of them, and drawn from too wide a social sphere.

However, a most unlooked-for acquaintance was to be thrust upon Fanny, and to charm and interest her so much that she was reinvigorated despite her initial hesitation. She wrote to Susan:

> Soon after we came, while I was finishing some letters, & quite alone, Mrs Ord's servant brought me word Lady Spencer would ask me how I did, if I was well enough to receive her. Of course, I hoped she might come upstairs.
>
> I have met her two or three times at my dearest Mrs Delany's, where I met also, with marked civilities from her – I was not, therefore, much amazed at this honour, though not the less obliged by it. I knew she was here, with her unhappy daughter, Lady Duncannon, whom she assiduously nurses, aided by her more celebrated other daughter, the Duchess of Devonshire.

This was no ordinary visit to Bath on the Spencers' part. Some months before, Lady Spencer's son-in-law, the Duke of Devonshire, had brought the extended family to Bath to help Harriet, Lady Duncannon recover from a recent dangerous illness. Though passed off as a miscarriage followed by pneumonia, her malady was rumoured to have resulted from a botched abortion, or else a suicide attempt by poisoning, brought on by an abusive husband. She was still weak, having to be carried from couch to carriage or chair. Not only to try the medicinal effects of Bath, but to escape from London scandal-mongering, were the Duke's motives in this wholesale removal of his family. He actually took an additional house in Marlborough Buildings solely for his infant son and his attendants, to which no tradesman was permitted for fear of introducing smallpox. Also in the party, besides the young children of the two sisters, was the Duchess's friend and Duke's mistress Lady Elizabeth Foster, together with six year old Caroline St Jules, offspring of their guilty liaison, unacknowledged and yet common knowledge to everybody including the horrified Fanny.

Indeed, everything about this group of women was calculated to horrify and alienate a member of the respectable middle classes like Fanny. They were stupendously rich, yet perpetually running up debts of thousands of pounds at the gaming tables, and lax about paying their tradesmen; they engaged in serial adultery – even at that moment, Georgiana, who had given the Duke two daughters and at last the longed-for heir, was pregnant by another man, Charles Grey; and they were Whigs. Fanny had been at Court during the Regency crisis just a few years before, when the Whigs had strongly promoted the Prince of Wales' precipitate moves to be made Regent. To George III, Queen Charlotte and all who revered them, like Fanny, Whigs were the enemy. And of all Whigs, Georgiana was, as Fanny herself termed her, 'head of the opposition public', famous – or infamous – for her campaigning and political intrigues at the highest level.

Fanny might have been expected to shun such a group, as much as common politeness allowed; and indeed she did at first conduct herself towards Lady Duncannon, and even more Lady Elizabeth Foster, with, as she herself termed it, 'coldness and reserve' (which probably amused them and confirmed their view of her as hopelessly *bourgeoise*). But despite herself she was won over – by Lady Spencer's apparent seriousness, by Harriet's softness and gratitude for the services rendered her by her family, and by Georgiana's charm. Lady Elizabeth never succeeded in conquering Fanny's revulsion, reminded as she always by little Caroline of her ladyship's adultery with the Duke. Fanny was inclined to believe, erroneously, that Georgiana was 'secretly hurt, offended & unhappy' about Lady Elizabeth's presence in the household. This is how Fanny described Georgiana after a second meeting, at which Lady Elizabeth was not present:

> I now saw the Duchess far more lively in her spirits, & consequently, far more lovely in her person; vivacity is so much her characteristic, that her style of beauty requires it indispensably; the beauty, indeed, dies away without it. I now saw how her fame for personal charm had been obtained; the expression of her smiles is so very sweet, & has an ingenuousness & openness so

singular, that, taken in those moments, not the most rigid critic could deny the justice of her personal celebrity.

The epithet charming, Fanny concluded, might have been coined for the Duchess.

Georgiana, Duchess of Devonshire, by Sir Martin Archer Shee. *(Devonshire Collection, Chatsworth. Reproduced by courtesy of the Chatsworth Settlement Trustees)*

To what extent did birth and breeding play a part in Fanny's seduction by the Spencers – either by endowing them with the instinctive knowledge of how to behave appropriately towards a person so different from themselves as Fanny was; or by inclining her to overlook their faults because of who they were? A product of the 18th century, and the daughter of a man notoriously susceptible to flattery and attention from above, Fanny struggled to come to a just assessment of the Spencers. She was certainly either more susceptible, or more generous, than Mrs Ord, whose disapproval of them was unmitigated, both on moral and on party political grounds; a 'rooted aversion', Fanny called it. 'Poor Mrs Ord is quite in dismay at this acquaintance, & will believe no good of them.' It caused awkwardness between the travelling companions, but despite her own reservations, Fanny found herself unable to decline any invitation to join the Spencers.

They were remarkably attentive to her. One of the reasons, doubtless, was that they were bored, and Fanny was a novelty. They had been in Bath already for weeks, and by 1791 it was no longer the fashionable place it had been, so company of their own kind was limited (a situation the Duke had depended upon). They seem to have chosen their invitations with care. At the beginning of the acquaintance with Fanny, Lady Spencer took her to a Sunday School at the Abbey of which she was patroness, and the next day to visit a school for the poor where six little girls were given new clothes to mark the sixth birthday of Lady Harriet Cavendish. These were visits well calculated to please Fanny. Not that she was not without her own worldly concerns when invited to the birthday party. This would be the first time she would be in company with not only Lady Spencer but her daughters and granddaughters. Would she be fine enough? 'You must give me leave to make one enquiry', she managed to say as she took leave of Lady Spencer the day before, 'which is – whether any lady besides the six little girls will be expected to come in a new gown? – for I am out of all visiting trappings'. It was an elegant way to frame the enquiry, but a surely a betrayal of Fanny's fundamental insecurity. She might feel superior to these people morally, but socially she was anxious not to appear a figure of fun.

They were much too well bred to allow any such contempt, supposing them to feel any, to appear. After this meeting with them all Fanny summed up her responses:

> I came away impressed with the most mixt sensations of pain & pleasure. The terrible stories circulated of the miserable misconduct of part of this community made me shudder at their powers of pleasing; & the excellence of the behaviour & manner I witnessed, contradicted them all & rendered these objects of defamation patterns of virtue!

Poor Lady Duncannon, instead of being benefited by the waters, caught a cold from bathing in them, and was advised to try the air of Clifton. Together with the Duchess and Lady Elizabeth, she was installed in lodgings in Hotwells. Georgiana travelled to Bath every day, some 13 miles each way, to see her son in Marlborough Buildings, returning to Bristol to spend the evenings with her sick sister – all this much to Fanny's satisfaction. Lady Spencer remained in Bath in charge of those of her grandchildren who had been left behind. What time she had left from these cares she devoted, according to Fanny, to 'pious works'.

Lady Duncannon's removal was made on 3rd September, and on the 10th, Fanny and Mrs Ord were to make their departure. 'Three days before we left Bath', Fanny wrote, 'as I was coming with Mrs Ord from the Pump Room, we encountered a Chair, from which a lady repeatedly kissed her hand to me. I was too near-sighted to distinguish who she was, till coming close, & a little stopt by more people, she put her face to the glass, & said, "How d'y'do? How d'y'do?" and I recollected the Duchess of Devonshire'. Moreover, 'The last person I saw was Lady Spencer, who, late in the evening, & in the midst of our packing, came & sat for a very pleasant half hour.' As a result of the Spencers' notice of her, Fanny left Bath feeling that it had been a visit compounded of pain and pleasure.

Mixing with the Spencers, weighing up their attractions and their shortcomings, had restored the novelist's interest in her fellow creatures. And certainly the visit had been good for her health, which had been the original objective. The Bath waters, Fanny wrote, were usually prescribed for six weeks, though she and Mrs Ord stayed only three. Despite the difficulties of walking through mud and debris between Queen Square and the Pumproom, Fanny had drunk the waters religiously morning and noon every day of her visit. There is no suggestion that she bathed in them like Lady Duncannon. Fanny believed the waters agreed with her, and that she was, as she wrote to Hetty, 'recovering apace'. She left Bath feeling happier and livelier than she could have imagined possible on leaving London six weeks before.

Had she known that it would be 24 years before she would see Bath again, and that when she did so it would be as a wife and mother, she would surely have been astonished.

4. Resident of Bath, 1815-1818

The Wanderer

When Fanny Burney left Bath in September 1791, it was to pay a long visit to her sister Susan Phillips, now living at Mickleham in Surrey. It was during a second visit to Susan, towards the end of the following year or early in 1793, that Fanny met the man who was to become her husband. Alexandre d'Arblay was one of a group of French emigrés who had found temporary shelter at Juniper Hall, a large house on the outskirts of the village. Susan, who had been educated partly in France, and therefore spoke excellent French, soon befriended the exiles. When Fanny came to stay she was naturally introduced, and since she did *not* speak excellent French, she and Alexandre offered to teach one another their respective languages, a ploy which soon led to their falling mutually in love.

In fleeing the Terror, Alexandre, an army officer loyal to the monarchy, had forfeited all his property. He had also lost his means of livelihood. Not only without fortune or prospects, Alexandre was also of course a Catholic, and a native of the country now at war with England. No wonder that Charles Burney was horrified when he found out what was happening. But this time Fanny would not give way. To marry the man she loved, she was prepared to face penury and the world's disapproval. Indeed she seems almost to have welcomed them, as proof that her love was disinterested and noble. Glorying in this moral high ground, it seems not to have occurred to her that she was acting very little differently from Mrs Thrale a decade before.

Charles gave his consent but not his blessing to the marriage. He remained fearful that Fanny's pension from the British Court of £100 per year, the couple's only secure income, would be withdrawn in high dudgeon at Fanny's temerity in marrying a citizen of France. It was not. Fanny married in July 1793, given away by her brother since her father refused to be present. She was 41, Alexandre 39. In December 1794, their only child was born. Given the English form of his father's Christian name, he was usually known as Alex.

Alexandre d'Arblay, artist unknown, c.1793. *(Reproduced by courtesy of the National Portrait Gallery, London)*

The need for money was now desperate and, showing her mettle, Fanny now sat down to write herself into a nest-egg. Her third novel, *Camilla, or a Picture of Youth*, was published in

1796 by the risky but potentially lucrative subscription method, whereby subscribers were induced by the author's fame to pay for the book in advance; what was left after production costs were met was the author's profit. Fanny's fame was such that she raised over £2,000 this way, almost ten times what the sale of her last novel's copyright had brought her, and enough to pay for the construction of Camilla Cottage in West Humble, Surrey. (The subscribers got to have their names printed in the first edition; one was Miss J Austen of Steventon in Hampshire, just 20 at the time.)

Fanny's marriage was a very happy one; she and Alexandre turned out to be true friends and real partners in all their ventures and difficulties. Emotionally stable and mutually supportive, they were yet to have an eventful married life, calling out Fanny's best qualities of steadfastness and courage. Refusing to repine over their lack of worldly prosperity, she was to be forever grateful that, at an age when marriage prospects seemed over, she had actually found such a soul-mate.

After years of poverty in the cottage (Alexandre grew vegetables as an essential part of their domestic economy), they were tempted by the Peace of Amiens in 1802 to cross the Channel in an attempt to regain the d'Arblay property. The play that Fanny had written the previous year, *A Busy Day*, was put aside, never to be performed in her lifetime. Trapped by the resumption of war, the d'Arblays spent the next ten years in Paris. During this time Fanny underwent a mastectomy *without anaesthetic*, on her own bed at home. Her detailed account of this ordeal is the most harrowing episode in her Journals. But she survived to live another 30 years.

In 1812, to save 18-year-old Alex from being conscripted into the French army, which was just then embarking on its Russian campaign, Fanny contrived to smuggle him back into England, and to deposit him with her relations while she returned to her husband's side. After Napoleon's first defeat in 1814, both d'Arblays paid a visit to England just in time to be with Fanny's father before he died. She also took the opportunity to see her fourth and last novel, *The Wanderer*, through the press, before returning, though with some reluctance, at her husband's desire to France.

With the return of Napoleon, Alexandre, though by now well advanced into middle age, and not fully recovered from a horrible injury to the chest he had received from the shaft of a cart in Calais on their return to France the previous November, took up arms on behalf of the French loyalists (a small anti-Napoleonic army co-operating with the British to defeat the upstart and restore the Bourbons). In the spring of 1815, her husband having left Paris under military orders, Fanny too was forced to flee France for Belgium, accompanied only by a female friend, and disguised as a *femme du chambre*. The d'Arblays met up in Brussels, but were soon separated again when Alexandre was dispatched to Trèves, as a result of which he narrowly missed seeing action at Waterloo. But extraordinarily, Fanny, with her knack of witnessing key events in history, found herself as close to the combat as it was possible for a woman to be. The 'piles of dead – heaps, masses, hills of Dead! French, English, Belge & Prussian, are horrible', she wrote, witnessing the mass burials. Her descriptions of the scene before and after battle were to be used by Thackeray when he was writing *Vanity Fair*.

A further terrifying journey undertaken alone, lasting six days, at last reunited Fanny with Alexandre, whom she found on the verge of death. He had been badly kicked by a horse and the neglected leg wound turned to septicaemia. It was a month before he could be moved. Re-entering France, the d'Arblays found the country in a state of moral and physical devastation in the aftermath of crushing defeat. Alexandre could not but agree with Fanny that the best place to regain his health was England. And of all England, Fanny had set her heart on living in Bath.

A good place to be poor in

Health and economy were Fanny's two reasons for choosing Bath, besides the simple fact that she liked the place. She had great faith in the efficacy of the Bath waters. The couple landed at Dover on 17th October 1815 and, sparing only a fortnight in London for seeing relations and ordering their financial affairs, they set out for Bath on 2nd November. 'The lameness of my poor limping partner makes us very desirous to get to our winter

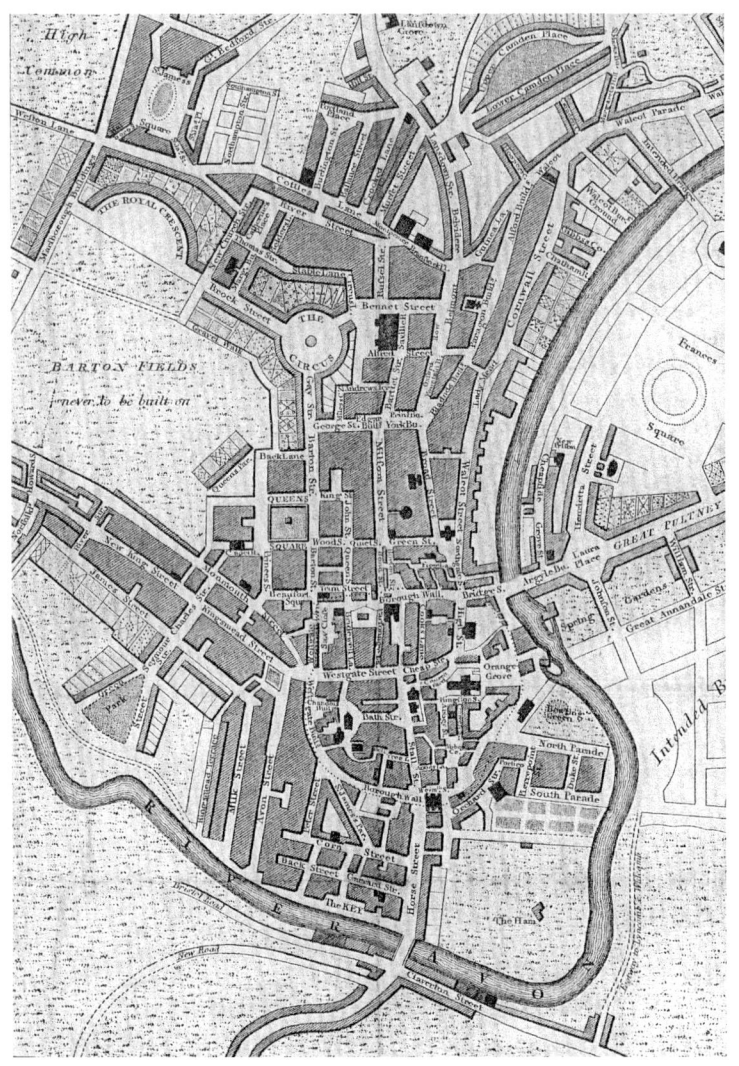

Part of a map of Bath, dated 1815, the year in which Fanny Burney and her husband took up residence in Bath.

abode, & to try the waters without loss of time', Fanny wrote during this fortnight, 'especially as we travel in an open carriage'.

This uncomfortable measure was presumably endured for the few shillings it saved. Fortunately when the time came to set out the day was fine. Roads were so much improved since 1780, when the Thrales spent four days getting from London to Bath, that the present journey was accomplished in just one day. 'The day fine, the road excelling, the views & remaining verdure admirable', Fanny noted cheerfully in her pocket book, enjoying as so many returned travellers do the greenness of the English countryside.

The d'Arblays' financial situation on their return to Bath is known in some detail. At first *The Wanderer* had sold well, on the strength of Fanny's name, and the (mistaken) expectation from the title that it would describe something of the author's own wanderings in Napoleonic France. But most readers were disappointed, and sales soon tailed off. Nevertheless, it brought Fanny £1,500 which, together with the proceeds from Camilla Cottage, amounting to £700 (the d'Arblays found they had never had title to the land it was built on), was invested to yield £300 p.a. Their only additional income was the continuing royal pension of £100. (Fanny, collecting this pension for almost 50 years, received far more this way than ever she had in salary. Her five years' court servitude turned out to have been an excellent bargain.) Two months after the return to Bath, Alexandre was granted by a grateful Louis XVIII the rank and title of Lt. General, together with right to half pay. But actually receiving any money from the impoverished French coffers was another matter. On little more than £400 p.a., therefore, the d'Arblays had to keep a roof over their heads and support their son Alex, now an undergraduate at Cambridge.

Before their arrival, lodgings had been taken for them at 23 Rivers Street by two nieces resident in Bath. Maria Bourdois, a widow, and her unmarried sister Sophia Burney, who had a home together at 5 Ainslie's Belvedere, off Lansdown Hill, were two of the many children of Fanny's eldest sister, Hetty, and her husband (and cousin) Charles Rousseau Burney. The lodgings had been engaged only for a month, which was fortunate, as they turned out to be much too expensive for the d'Arblays' budget on account of their proximity to the Assembly Rooms.

5 Ainslie's Belvedere

The very next morning Fanny set off with Sophy to look for something cheaper. She spent the next four days house-hunting, at the same time renewing her acquaintance with the city. Her pocket-book, in which only the briefest of entries were made, notes on Friday 3rd November: 'enchanted with this beautiful city'; on Saturday: 'How glorious in noble taste is the Royal Crescent!'; on Sunday: 'How delicately finished is the Circus!' and on Monday: 'How strikingly beautiful in every style of picturesque effect is Cambden [*sic*] place & Prospect place!'.

Not that the d'Arblays aspired to any of these addresses, of course. They settled for lodgings at 23 Great Stanhope Street, which they took initially from 29th November until the first of May. Fanny described the situation to her brother James:

> We have had great difficulty in finding comfortable & pleasant lodgings at a reduced price: but we have at last succeeded. They are in GREAT Stanhope Street; as it is called, not, by any means, from being of a magnitude or magnificence to merit

the epithet, but because they have judged proper to name LITTLE Stanhope Street a mere lane which is by its side. But its principal recommendation is a beautiful view of a noble hill from the back apartments. We are not upon the heights, which would be too bleak for the Winter: nor too near the pump-room, which might be too warm for the Summer. I think it a situation that must be salubrious & agreeable for every season. It is within a few yards of a delicious Winter's walk, called The Norfolk Crescent. I ought to have some partiality to such a vicinity [a joke: Fanny had been born in Norfolk]: & indeed, while shaded by the charming building, it is always dry, except *during* rain, from the constant current of air & the great breadth of pavement; & it is open to views of such varied beauty & richness that I anticipate an almost endless delight from its inviting nearness.

23 Great Stanhope Street

To her other brother, Charles, Fanny wrote in similar vein that their house 'is very pleasantly situated; not upon the heights, which would be too bleak for Winter, yet not in the old town, which would be too shut up for those who love to watch the opening buds of early spring'.

Great Stanhope Street, long and narrow, was then on the western edge of Bath, near both the river Avon (after it had made its curve round the city) and the road to Bristol, and not far from some of the most insalubrious, working-class streets in the city – but these Fanny never mentions. Like all low-lying parts of the city then, it was liable to damps, but had the advantage of a level approach to the Pump-room and city centre. Its houses were of a very moderate size, suited to respectable but not fashionable people. The d'Arblays occupied the first and second floors of the house; their landlords, Mr & Mrs Brenan, occupying the ground floor and basement. The d'Arblays made their drawing room on the first floor at the back, to take advantage of the southerly prospect and view to the hills on the other side of the Avon. The front room on that floor was Fanny's bedroom. Above the drawing room was Alexandre's bedroom, with a room for Alex above Fanny's, and a walk-in closet lined with shelves which they called their book-room.

Higher rents were charged everywhere in Bath during the winter season. From the evidence it would seem that the d'Arblays paid not less than £5 per week from April to September, and for the rest of the year considerably more. Almost their entire income, therefore, went on lodgings, leaving very little over for such contingencies as doctors' bills. Board and service seem to have been included in the rent; that is, Mrs Brenan or her servant cleaned their rooms, cooked their meals, made their fires and emptied their chamber pots. Whether coals and washing were charged as extras is not known. And although their meals were cooked and served, the fact that Alexandre resumed his old occupation of growing vegetables (for which he rented what we would today know as an allotment) suggests either that they had to provide their own food, or, perhaps more likely, that Mrs Brenan made them an allowance for the produce.

Fanny was convinced of the economic advantages of living in Bath. In April she wrote:

Bath will, I think, & trust, & hope, & believe, be our ultimate place of residence: There is no place I have yet seen where the inconveniences of a limited fortune are so little felt, nor where the people at large are so civilised. As there are no manufactures, & scarcely any commerce, here, the rapacity of wealth has not infected men's minds, and thought [with] the mercantile value of human intercourse, by the prospect of gain or fear of loss. Equipage, servants, table, jewels, though *here*, as everywhere, very desirable, are not *here* requisite … There is something nearer to independence from the shackles of fortuitous circumstances in the society of Bath than I have ever witnessed elsewhere.

'The people are so honest', she wrote in January 1817, 'that we never fasten our windows & barely our doors at night, & so civil, that I have passed here more than a year without once witnessing either disturbance or rudeness during the day.' 23 Great Stanhope Street was to remain the d'Arblays' home for the whole of their time in Bath, as they kept renewing the lease, knowing that nowhere else would better suit both their tastes and their purse. Summing up all the advantages offered by Bath for people like themselves, she wrote to another friend in May 1816:

We are much pleased with Bath & I hope it will be our permanent residence. It has a thousand coaxing recommendations to folks of small pecuniary means. No carriage is requisite; the market is good and reasonable; firing is deliciously attainable; Town & Country are united; health or pleasure bring hither sooner or later almost everybody; it is a great resort of foreigners; all the eminent artists visit it occasionally. To walk in the streets is as safe, easy & clean as to walk in a courtyard. The people are so honest, so innocent, that bars and bolts, even at night, seem superfluous;

> as there is neither commerce nor manufactory, there is neither bankruptcy nor ruin; as people come hither for health or for pleasure, not for business or profit, money loses its balance; & character & conduct suffice for independence & equality; AND, invisibility even to a next door neighbour, never gives offence.
>
> Our situation is excellent; it is apart from the bleak of the hills, the currents of sharp air in its avenues, & the oppressive damps of the baths. The prospect from our back-rooms is beautiful; & our apartments are clean, neat & pretty.

As for Bath's advantages to health, however, which she had so much depended upon, these did not turn out all she had hoped. Alexandre's wound had opened up in all the travelling before they reached Bath, and for several weeks he was ordered not to walk, thereby preventing visits to the Pump-room. Then for the first few weeks of 1816, severe cold weather – Fanny speaks of both her ink and her fingers being frozen – and a series of bad colds kept them both indoors. When at last they could get out, Fanny wrote, she intended to drink the waters and her husband to have the warm water pumped over his wound, as recommended by his physician. But as late as June 1816 she had to report that 'I am well – but have never yet been quite free enough from all shadow of cold to try the fortifying effects of the Bath waters', while as for Alexandre, 'The lameness amends; but the limb is weakened, & the smallest exertion, or accident, is felt, still, severely!'

In fact Alexandre was never to be completely well again, one trouble succeeding another. It seems likely that the cancer from which he was to die in 1818 was, though unsuspected, already taking its toll as they so hopefully began their new life. Fanny's years as a resident of Bath, though they brought her many quiet pleasures, were to be plagued by three sources of anxiety: her husband's health, their financial situation, and whether Alex, who remained strangely childlike and irresponsible into adulthood, would ever work hard enough to obtain his degree.

'I thought it a Paradise'

Fanny's first impressions of Bath after a quarter century's absence were expressed in the somewhat high-flown language which she presumably judged suited to the grandeur of her correspondent, the Princess Elizabeth. Every new visit to Bath, Fanny wrote, a month after their return,

> presents new wonders that gaily invite & richly recompense a new survey. It is at this very time, though near the end of November, in a state of luxurious beauty that would baffle description, and almost surpass even the ideal perfection of a painter's fancy. Hills rising above hills, here smiling with verdure, there shadowed with woods, here undulating to catch the eye to distant prospects, & there striking with noble edifices, terminate almost every street, & spread in broad exhilarating views before every Crescent, with a variety of attraction, from local positions or accidents, that are endless in their effects to elevate, or please. Our admiration never tires, though our power to gratify it, by continually mounting or descending, are by no means equally invulnerable to fatigue.

We can imagine the d'Arblays slowly walking the streets of Bath, arm-in-arm, somewhat like that other companionable and self-sufficient middle-aged couple, Admiral and Mrs Croft, in *Persuasion*, set in this very same year of 1815. (Fanny's eulogies on the cheapness of Bath testify to Jane Austen's knowledge of Bath's changing social ethos in having Mr Shepherd recommend it as a place of residence to Sir Water Elliot, a gentleman distressed for money.) Just like the Crofts, the d'Arblays would chance upon their friends in the streets, shops or Pump-room – they soon came to have 'an immensely extensive acquaintance' in the city – but would happily return to their own snug quarters for the afternoon and evening. The d'Arblays took their dinner at four, never dined out, and only exceptionally made any evening visit.

They were content with one another's company, and the tranquil pleasures of reading and writing over their own fireside. Fanny had sent for 'an immense hoard of papers: 3 trunks full, chiefly MSS & Letters of my dearest Father' which had been left behind in France. These she began sorting with a view – eventually accomplished, though not until long after she had left Bath – of writing his biography. As ever, she kept up an extensive correspondence which must have occupied much of her time. The d'Arblays do not seem to have stinted themselves of books, judging from the number of bookshelves which had to be removed when they vacated their lodgings. They patronised two booksellers, Barratt and Son of 17 Bond Street and Upham's of The Walks. Both these establishments were also private libraries, where for a modest subscription, in addition to purchasing, consulting or borrowing books, the daily newspaper could be read. Perhaps Alexandre would sometimes spend an hour or two here while his wife paid calls on her female friends. Another of his daytime resources was gardening, which he kept up as long as he was able, first renting a plot between Great Stanhope Street and the river, later exchanging this for an allotment on the healthier but not too elevated hillside of Crescent Fields, below the Royal Crescent.

Fanny's long-standing interest in the theatre could now occasionally be indulged. In 1805 the old theatre in Orchard Street, which she had patronised so often with the Thrales, had closed, to be replaced by a handsome new building in Sawclose, on Fanny's side of the city. As a celebrity, she was actually offered free tickets by the management to use whenever she wished; but her lifelong dislike of receiving something for nothing, or of feeling herself the object of charity, prevented her from accepting – just as it prevented her from accepting dinner invitations which she could not reciprocate (and just as she had shrunk from accepting gifts from the Thrales). Economy and poor health meant the d'Arblays could not often attend the theatre, but they did see several performances, including Edmund Kean in *Hamlet*, John Kemble in both *Coriolanus* and *King John*, and Fanny Kemble in *The Way to Keep Him* and *The Devil to Pay*. One of the purposes in building the new theatre had been to provide spacious approaches for carriages and chairs both front and back, in

Sawclose and Beaufort Street. As one who well remembered the crush in Orchard Street, Fanny was appreciative. 'We had quiet places kept for us, & the entrance and exits at the Bath Theatre are as easy as those into a private house', she marvelled.

Another indulgence was the long-term rental of a seat, with her name on it, in the private Octagon Chapel, off Milsom Street. When Fanny was away from Bath for three months in the summer of 1817, she was able to confer the right to this seat to whomsoever she chose. The Octagon Chapel, opened in 1767, was noted for the elegance and comfort of its interior, and was the most fashionable of Bath's six proprietary chapels.

Fanny had never had much interest in clothes, and it was no hardship for her to lag behind the latest fashions – as she presumably did; and on the whole she appears not to have noticed such things. But she did make one amusing observation on a group of three young ladies, daughters of the Earl of Kentore, who had been brought up 'in a distant & retired province of Scotland':

> I am amused by meeting them in the streets of Bath, which they perambulate so oddly, & so underdressed, compared with the magnificent costume of the Bath walking Belles, in general, that they may really pass, to those by whom they are unknown, for little Housemaids: *lady's* maids, commonly, being more showily attired *even* than their mistresses.

Both summers of their Bath residence – that is, 1816 and 1817 – the d'Arblays hoped to travel together to France for Alexandre to try to collect his arrears of pay. In both cases, he ended up going alone, so that Fanny could be with Alex to make sure he worked. In 1816 mother and son remained in Bath, but in 1817 Alex was offered free tutorials with some other Cambridge men during the vacation at Ilfracombe, on the North Devon coast. Though he was by then 22 years of age, Fanny insisted on taking lodgings there with him. Since two sets of lodgings could not be afforded, 23 Great Stanhope Street was given up for three months. In order that the Brenans could let the rooms to others, the d'Arblays' possessions had to be packed up and stored partly in the garret, partly with an obliging friend who lived in the Royal Crescent. Alexandre returned from France in October neither richer nor, as he had hoped, restored to health by his native air.

Fanny had no faith in his native air; she continued to place hers in the waters and amenities of Bath, which she herself enjoyed so much, and which she was convinced also suited her husband's constitution. Right up to the end she was in denial, refusing to believe that her husband, two years younger than herself and the rock on which she had leant for quarter of a century, could possibly die and leave her.

She described him as being 'always lame, & terribly susceptible of pain & uneasiness at every false or hasty step, and at any uneven ground'. Their walks became confined to the immediate vicinity of their home (happily Norfolk Crescent was so close) and eventually the gardening had to be given up. An acquaintance on whom Fanny called in 1817 wrote: 'The poor man is now a miserable object with the jaundice; and I fear they are far from comfortable in their circumstances, and are living with the greatest economy, to enable them to support their son genteelly at the University.' But Fanny wasn't the pitiful figure in company this might suggest: the same letter reported her as being 'very amiable in her manners' and willing and able to talk on a variety of amusing topics.

Later, looking back on those final three years of her marriage, Fanny was to write of Bath itself, which had consoled and comforted her through so much, 'I thought it a Paradise'.

A literary coincidence

In her pocket books for these years Fanny noted the books she read, and her judgement of them. It is a sorry truth that she makes no mention of any of Jane Austen's novels, all six of which were published either just preceding, or actually during, Fanny's residence in Bath. This is all the more odd in that in Bath Fanny renewed her acquaintance with a relation of Jane Austen who was herself a published novelist, and would surely have mentioned the novels. Cassandra Cooke was the author of *Battleridge*, a novel with a Civil War setting but a fashionably gothic flavour, published in 1799.[1] She was first cousin to Jane Austen's mother and her husband, the Reverend Samuel Cooke, Rector of Great Bookham in Surrey, was Jane Austen's godfather. Jane was close to the Cookes and their children, staying with them in the Great Bookham Rectory, and associating with the family when they visited Bath during the Austens' own period of residence, 1801-1806. When the d'Arblays lived in Surrey the Cookes were near neighbours, and Jane Austen's godfather had actually christened Fanny d'Arblay's son. Now, in the Spring of 1816, the Cookes spent two months in Bath and exchanged visits with the d'Arblays, as they did again when they stayed in the city in 1817. 'The Cookes I saw as often as I could', wrote Fanny, regarding them as true old friends for whom she was happy to break her self-imposed rule of socialising as little as possible.

If it would seem almost impossible that Cassandra Cooke would have refrained from mentioning the novels of her young relation, it is also intriguing to speculate whether information flowed in the other direction; whether Jane Austen herself heard from the Cookes about their renewed acquaintance with the novelist whom she had admired and learnt from perhaps more than any other in her formative years. By the Spring of 1816 Jane Austen was working on the Bath chapters of *Persuasion* – the novel was finished in August of that year. At the very least Jane Austen must have been amused to hear how like her own Crofts the d'Arblays were in their habits and self-sufficiency, and how intriguingly their quest for economy echoed, if not resembled, that of her character Sir Walter Elliot.

Fanny might also have heard of the new novelist from her sister Sarah Harriet Burney, who was in Bath in the autumn of 1816. Sarah Harriet was herself a novelist, publishing five novels altogether including her first, *Clarentine*, which Jane Austen is known to have read three times (though she found it did not bear a third reading). In the early part of 1816, Sarah Harriet's publisher Henry Colburn sent her a copy of the newly published *Emma*. In writing to thank him, Sarah Harriet said that it had 'afforded me much amusement'. To a niece also reading the novel, she wrote, 'I have read no story book with such glee, since the days of 'Waverley' and 'Mannering' [Walter Scott's first two novels]

[1] Marshall, Judith, 'Battleridge' in *The Jane Austen Society Report for 1997*.

and, by the same author as 'Emma', my prime favourite of all modern novels, 'Pride and Prejudice'.[1] With such enthusiasm, is it possible that in visiting her sister – and sister novelist – only six months later she failed to mention or recommend them?

Mrs Piozzi

Almost the first social call made by Fanny after her arrival in Bath was on her estranged friend Hester Thrale, now Mrs Piozzi, and widowed for the second time. Despite everybody's prognostications her marriage seems to have brought her the happiness she expected. The Piozzis had returned from Italy in 1787 and, building themselves a country house in Hester's native Wales, had spent part of almost every winter in Bath. Gabriel Piozzi suffered from gout, which eventually brought him a lingering, painful death in 1809. Mrs Piozzi then rather rashly made over her Welsh property to one of his nephews, Italian of course by birth, but educated at her expense in England and given her own maiden surname of Salusbury. The house at Streatham had been left by Henry Thrale to his four surviving daughters, but his widow had a life interest in it, and its repairs and upkeep fell on her. Just at this time she could find no tenant for it, and this combination of circumstances made her, for the first time in her life, extremely short of ready money. Though she had always been used to handsome lodgings in Bath, at the time of Fanny's arrival in the city, she was reduced to living in a pair of rooms in New King Street at two guineas a week. This location, as Fanny remarked, was hardly 20 houses in a straight line from her own home, and she knew she must call.

The two women had not spoken to each other for 31 years, though they had heard of one another's doings through mutual friends. Fanny still corresponded with Queeney, who had married for the first time at 44, and was now Lady Keith. Fanny approached Hester with trepidation, and was met with what she perceived as petrifying coldness. They who had once been so close, now spent half an hour in formal, meaningless conversation, and came away both feeling as aggrieved and sore as ever.

[1] Clark, Lorna J (editor), *The Letters of Sarah Harriet Burney*, The University of Georgia Press, 1997.

Mrs Piozzi was not to stay in her 'dingy lodgings' (the description is her own) for long. The following May she raised a considerable sum by the sale of Streatham's contents. Fanny was saddened when she thought of the break-up of that once glittering place, but thrilled that her brother Charles made a successful bid for the portrait of their father commissioned by Henry Thrale from Sir Joshua Reynolds. Mrs Piozzi was more successful in finding a tenant for the property now it was unfurnished. Wealthy again, she moved into lodgings at 8 Gay Street, which remained her home for the rest of her life. The house, the most ornate one in the street, is now marked by a plaque. In January 1820, to celebrate what she called her 80th birthday, though it was actually her 79th, she threw a party for 600 people in the Assembly Rooms, thereby impoverishing herself for a second time, though by then it hardly mattered. She died in Bristol in 1821.

Fanny's sisters and Bath

Except for Susan, who had died in 1800, all Fanny's sisters lived in Bath at some period of their lives, and all visited the city while she was a resident there.

Sarah Harriet was poorer even than Fanny, never having more than £100 per year secure income; her writing occasionally brought in a little more, but never earned her as much as Fanny's. She never married. After devoting many years to keeping house for Dr Burney, she spent the rest of her life drifting about by herself, including several years in Florence; she would have spells of hiring herself out as companion or governess, but more often she occupied meagre lodgings alone with her maid. In the summer and autumn of 1816 she spent several months in Malvern Wells for her health. (In the town itself she had to pay two guineas a week for a sitting room, bedroom and garret for the maid. After a few weeks of this she moved out into the country, where she could rent a cottage for one guinea, and ride into town on a donkey.) On her way back to London she broke her journey in Bath, staying with Maria and Sophy at Ainslie's Belvedere.

Twenty years later Sarah Harriet made Bath her home. From March 1834 to June 1841 she had a room in a ladies' boardinghouse at 22 Henrietta Street. Sarah Harriet was, indeed, typical of the population of Bath by this period, and indeed for the next hundred years: predominantly female, constrained by a combination of slender means and jealously guarded gentility. More intellectual than most, at least in her own estimation, she disdained her fellow-lodgers, 'persons who have never been beyond Clifton, or perhaps Weston-super-Mer'. How different from the days of the Blue Stockings! Even Fanny was doubtful whether the Bath of the 1830s was right for her restless sister: 'She will tire of its monotonous composure', she wrote. In 1841 Sarah Harriet moved to Cheltenham, where she was happier, for the remaining three years of her life.

Fanny's sister Charlotte had been the first to make Bath her home, living there with her invalid second husband from 1803 until his death in 1805. Charlotte was now living in Richmond with her unmarried children. By her first marriage she had three children and by her second one son, Ralph Broome, known as Dolph. Born in 1801, his health had always given cause for alarm, and by the spring of 1817 he was seriously ill – almost certainly of consumption, though his doctors did not admit as much at the time. Nevertheless, they advised his mother to take him to the south coast to live, perhaps for several years. On 18th April the little party of mother, son and married sister Charlotte Barrett set off for Sidmouth. Travelling painfully slowly, they took five days to reach Bath, where they paused. Fanny found them lodgings just a few doors away, at 17 Great Stanhope Street. Here, on 27th April, just four days after his arrival, Dolph died. Though he had been so long ill, his mother was totally unprepared for his death. The only consolation to Fanny was that Dolph had not died on the way to Bath, or between Bath and Sidmouth, but where his mother had two of her sisters to support her. For not only Fanny, but the eldest sister, Esther, were now residents of Bath.

Esther, or Hetty, and her husband Charles Rousseau Burney, had paid a long visit to Bath from 9th May to 27th July 1816 for treatment for the arthritis afflicting her hands. She seems to have found some relief. With living so cheap, with two of their daughters already established in Bath, and now with Fanny there too, the couple decided to leave London and make Bath their permanent home. Both musicians by profession, but without

Dr Burney's talent for self-promotion, they had always been poor, unworldly and impractical. Of their eight children, six were living, including two daughters still at home. They returned to Bath in March 1817 and purchased 5 Lark Hall Place, a new house in the Regency style. On the eastern fringe of Bath, almost in the country at that time, it was very cheap, very rural, very charming, and very inaccessible, reached only by a narrow lane that ran directly behind the terrace. As Fanny wrote in May to Charlotte:

> Our sister & her excellent Mate dined with us last week, both as well & as blyth as on the day of their marriage [47 years before!]. Could they but ensure their present state for life, their situation would be agreeable as well as rural: but, otherwise, I tremble at the least illness that may demand physician or friend, so aloof from both is their dwelling.

In this spring season the little house was delightful, with its long front garden bisected by a footpath, and its peaceful location. The first floor front room had windows opening on to a small iron balcony. Despite being not only in the same town but the same parish, that of Walcot, Lark Hall Place was (and is) a full two and a half miles from Great Stanhope Street, so that visiting between the sisters required some effort, and was most feasible in summer. On 27th June Fanny paid such a visit, with her husband and son Alex, painting a charming picture for Charlotte:

> We spent the afternoon at Lark Hall Place, to meet there Maria and Sophy. My dear sister was all spirit and vivacity: Mr Burney, all tranquil enjoyment. Peace, rest, leisure, books, music, drawing & walking fill up his serene days, & repay the long toils of his meritorious life. Amelia [the youngest daughter] seems much pleased with her new dwelling; & my poor sister, who happily foresees neither sickness nor ennui, is the spirit and spring of the party … We drank tea [on] their pleasant balcony, & they all accompanied us half way home, at near 10 o'clock at night! The weather was beautiful.

5 Lark Hall Place. The original first-floor balcony, retained on neighbouring properties, has been lost.

By August, however, Fanny was writing to Alexandre, now in Paris, 'My sister Esther already begins to dread winter, from the confinement & humidity she has experienced during the recent rains! We judged but too well the precipitance of her taking a house out of the reach of assistance, medical or friendly, in bad weather. I am truly sorry her eyes open too late.' The house, like so many in Bath, was not proof against rain, and winters at Lark Hall Place certainly had their share of discomfort. But they all made the best of things and the saving grace, perhaps, was the daughters' house at the Belvedere, where they could always stay for the night, since it was impossible to get back from the centre of Bath to Lark Hall Place on winter evenings. As Fanny explained, in another delightful vignette of domestic Bath life, written in November:

> Our sister Esther & her faithful mate are both, in general, in amazing good health, & super-amazing spirits. They enjoy their happy retirement in a manner the most lively & rational. They have some friends near them, whom they like much, & by whom they are nearly adored, that they contrive to see often. They have music at pleasure, & Mr Burney keeps up his talent for drawing with as much constancy & skill as his still more rare powers in music, in which he remains truly astonishing. Amelia is greatly improved in conversation & deportment. Maria is still the prettiest of the tribe, & always smiling & pleasing. Sophy is considerably improved in health & looks; & all are gay & happy. Maria & Sophy frequently pass several days together at Lark Hall Place & when any concert, or peculiar attraction, draw Mr B & our sister to Bath, they have a room & a bed at the Belvedere. Without this arrangement they could ill & rarely meet in winter; but with it, it makes their joint houses social & enlivened.

Charles Rousseau Burney died in 1819, after only two years' residence in Bath. For seven more years Esther remained – one is tempted to say stuck it out – at Lark Hall Place. In the summer of 1825 her daughter Maria Bourdois was contemplating a move from Ainslie's Belvedere to somewhere lower down the town. Fanny took the opportunity to urge her sister, who was now 76, 'Might you not try to let your house, & descend a little also? For if said house is so cold in Winter & so dusty in Summer, it seems only desirable for Spring & Autumn. After the fears I have conceived for your dearly precious health from the damp, I should not cry to hear of a removal, pretty as is your house, pretty in the extreme for summer, to the eye – but how inadequate is that for the whole of a dwelling.'

The following year Esther did move, taking a house at 19 New King Street for £65 per annum. (Rentals had dropped considerably in ten years, reflecting the loss, by now almost total, of fashionable visitors to Bath.) Maria and Sophy meanwhile took up occupancy in 6 Queen Square. Esther told Charlotte that her daughters had 'got into a charming situation now – having removed from Ainslie's Belvedere to a good house in Queen Square – and my removal to New King's Street brings us to be neighbours, and furnishes us with many advantages, of which we were wholly deprived by my residence at Lark Hall Place – a distance of nearly 2 miles from Bath – which in Winter rendered our meeting very rare – & in bad weather impossible.' She continued, showing the sprightly nature which had blest her all her life, 'Conveyances there are – but it *has* happened to me to sit a whole evening at home – when engaged to an agreeable party or concert owing to the negligence or pre-engagements of the drivers of the carriages. But – then I had the pleasure allowed me of seeing myself dressed out in my silks & my satins – which – with the comfort of sitting by a good fire – while the storm raged – did really sometimes afford me consolation.'

Fanny, who had herself long left Bath, rejoiced in her sister's sensible removal, which also called forth some nostalgia:

> I know all that part of the city of Bath but too – too well! – ah! What a consolation would it have been to me had you inhabited that vicinity while my dwelling was in Stanhope Street! Pray tell me whether Madame de Somerey is still there, and whether your house is above or below hers, that I may figure you more precisely to my satisfaction.

All the backs of King Street are, more or less, remarkably pleasant. Poor Mrs Piozzi resided there when first I went to Bath in 1815.

Does Maria like her house? Queen Square is a delightful situation. I resided there when I visited Bath with Mrs Ord.

Esther remained in Bath until her death in 1832, when she was buried beside her husband in Batheaston churchyard.

Death of a princess

In November 1817 the citizens of Bath were much excited at the prospect of a royal visit. Old Queen Charlotte was making her first progress to a part of the kingdom without her husband, now ill, blind and senile. As with Fanny's sisters, health was the motivation. She was accompanied by her son the Duke of Clarence and by Princess Elizabeth, from whom Fanny learned of the projected visit before it was public knowledge.

Despite – or because of – having seen the Royal family at such close quarters all those years ago, Fanny was a staunch royalist. Always when writing to or about the royal family, her language takes on an inflated air. This is how she described Bath's reception of the Queen and Princess in a letter to Alex:

> The joy exhibited on Monday, when Her Majesty & Her Royal Highness arrived, was really extatic; the illumination was universal. The public offices were splendid; so were the tradespeople's who had promises, or hopes, of employment; the Nobles & Gentles were modestly gay, & the poor eagerly put forth their mite. But all was flattering, because voluntary. Nothing was induced by power, or forced by mobs. All was left to individual choice. Your Padre & I patrolled the principal streets, & were quite touched by the universality of the homage paid to the virtues & merit of our venerable Queen, upon this her first progress through any part of her domains by herself.

On the afternoon of Monday 3rd November, the royal party entered Bath by the London Road. Cheering crowds lined the way along Milsom Street, New Bond Street and Great Pulteney Street to New Sydney Place, where lodgings had been taken at numbers 103 and 93 for the Queen and her entourage. On Tuesday they were driven round the city to survey the principal sights, and on Wednesday and Thursday mornings the Queen was conveyed by sedan chair to the Pump-room, where she drank the waters. 'Such a bustle Bath never witnessed before', noted Mrs Piozzi that day, and the scene seemed set for a successful and popular visit. On Thursday afternoon there was to be an official reception at the Guildhall. The Queen was dressing for this when news came that her granddaughter Princess Charlotte, daughter of the Prince Regent and eventual heir to the throne, had given birth to a stillborn child after a very long labour. As Fanny described the Queen at that moment:

> She was having her diamonds placed on her head for the reception of the Mayor & Corporation of Bath, with an address upon the honour done to their city, & upon their hopes from the salutary spring she came to quaff. Her first thought was to issue orders for deferring this ceremony; but when she considered that all the members of the municipality must be assembled, & attired; & that the great dinner they had prepared to give to the Duke of Clarence for celebrating the festival, could only be postponed at an enormous & useless expense, she composed her spirits, & finished her regal decorations, & admitted the citizens of Bath – who were highly gratified by her condescension, & struck by her splendour, which, in compliment to their attention, was the same as she appeared in on the greatest occasions of outward presentation in the Capital. The Princess Elizabeth also was a blaze of jewels. And our good little Mayor (not 4 foot high) & Aldermen & Common Council men, were all transported.

The mayor was John Kitson, apothecary, 75 years old; he surely prepared for this reception as the summit of his career. During it, the course of British history changed. The Queen and Princess had retired to dine privately, but the Duke of Clarence was just beginning his dinner in the Guildhall when a second express came, forwarded from New Sydney Place, announcing the death of Princess Charlotte herself. She was just 21, had been married less than a year, and was the hope of the nation. Indeed, she was the only legitimate grandchild of George III and Queen Charlotte, despite their having had 15 children, of whom 13 survived into adulthood. This was a blow too great even for royal habits and training to withstand. The Guildhall was emptied within minutes, the royal party shut themselves up all next day (but the Queen sent Fanny a private note 'most graciously … to console me') and on Saturday they returned to Windsor. 'All Bath wore a face of mourning', wrote Fanny. 'The transition from gaiety & exultation was really awful.'

Before long the middle-aged princes were looking about for young wives, and fathering a batch of babies, of whom the Duke of Kent's daughter, Victoria, would one day succeed to the throne. And Fanny, already 65 at the time of the catastrophe, would live to see the beginning of this most unlooked-for reign.

Meanwhile, after the funeral, now more in need of the waters than ever, the old Queen returned to Bath, arriving on 24th November and staying nearly until Christmas. She commanded Alexandre to be presented to her at the Pump-room, which Fanny deemed an inexpressible honour, though by then he was so ill he could hardly stand. All the people to be so presented to her were arranged standing in a semi-circle before the Queen was carried in by sedan chair. She was then 'waited upon' with the Bath water, and drank and conversed with her own people, before rising and making her round. The grace with which she did this, in Fanny's opinion, was 'such as to carry off age, infirmity, sickness, diminutive & disproportioned stature, & ugliness, & to give to her, in defiance of such disadvantages, a power of charming & delighting that rarely has been equalled'. Alexandre, according to Fanny, 'forgot his pains in his desire to manifest his gratitude', but 'the Queen no sooner ceased to adress him, than the pains he had suppressed became intolerable, & he retreated back from the circle, & sunk upon a form next the wall! He could stand no longer – & we returned home to spend the rest of the day in bodily misery.'

Despite feeling so much needed at home, during the Queen's stay in Bath, Fanny wrote, 'Daily I go with my respectful & most warm enquiries to Sydney Place, whatever be the weather, and whatever the [price] of chair hire, & whatever my other calls: for it is at once my devoir & my earnest desire to know how the Bath beverage agrees with Her Majesty.' From information contained in the *Bath Guide* for 1817 it can be calculated that for a chair from Great Stanhope Street to New Sydney Place and back Fanny would have paid five shillings (25p) with an extra six pence (2$\frac{1}{2}$p) for each quarter of an hour's waiting in excess of half an hour – no small sum from her tight budget. Towards the end of the royal visit, the Queen sent two of her household, friends of Fanny's from her court days, to pay a call at Great Stanhope Street, as the Queen wished, Fanny discovered, 'to have some account of my habitation'.

A year later, and both the Queen and Alexandre were dead, and Fanny had left Bath for ever.

* * *

Alexandre d'Arblay died on 3rd May 1818, after months of suffering bravely borne. He knew and accepted that he was dying, and did everything possible to put his papers and affairs in order, and to advise Fanny how she might live without him. He was certain that she ought to leave Bath, giving as his reasons that she must try to get out into the world again. Perhaps he had never liked Bath as much as Fanny did, or as much as she persuaded herself he did. Though Esther's residence in Bath was a reason to stay there, Alexandre had suggested Fanny join forces with her other sister, Charlotte, like her a widow. This was discussed between the two women for some months after Alexandre's death, but both had ties to their children that kept them apart. For Fanny was sure that now her only purpose in life was to look after Alex. And Alex – who had actually got a good degree, after causing years of anxiety to his parents – was 'decidedly, & even ardently for a residence in London. And nothing so natural', Fanny allowed, listing its attractions for the young. 'Bath, in itself, & with his dear friends, he likes –

but Bath is not a place for a young man to begin life in: it is too confined to females & invalides.'

In September 1818 the two remaining d'Arblays left Bath to make their home in London. Fanny thought herself indifferent to place now her beloved partner was dead. Yet her swiftly succeeding contradictory phrases, in one of the last letters she wrote from the city, betray ambivalence and confusion. 'Alas!' she wrote, 'for me Bath has lost all charms! though were Alex content to abide in it, I should be led by a thousand fond feelings never to quit it. Yet HE to whom I refer in every thought, was of the opinion I would no longer live here.'

She settled down in London with Alex (who became Perpetual Curate of Camden) and with her own and her father's papers, poring over them most evenings and rarely stirring out of doors after nightfall. The cost of transport in London was beyond her means, and she fondly recalled the (relative) cheapness of the chairs in Bath. As late as 1825 she was hankering after Bath, the only place, she believed, where penurious, unattached women could live with 'dignity and independence'. She never visited Bath again, despite her sister Esther's residence there for a further 14 years, and later the residence of Sarah Harriet. However, letters from these sisters kept her in touch with developments in Bath virtually for the rest of her life. Her preference for the city was unquenchable, and in January 1824, when Alex paid a visit to his cousins Maria and Sophy at Ainslie's Belvedere, she responded to a letter of his: 'I am glad you now do justice to beautiful Bath – Brighton, with all its *agremens*, is not, as *town*, fit to be its handmaid. Nor is any City *I* have ever visited.' For a woman of her times Fanny was well-travelled, both in England and on the Continent, and it is a tribute both to the city and to her continued ability to take pleasure in her surroundings that in 1824 as in 1780 she could use the same word, 'beautiful', to describe Bath. No matter that in the 44 years intervening both she and it had changed and aged considerably, both going out of fashion together.

St Swithin's Church, Walcot

5. The d'Arblays & St Swithin's

Fanny Burney, her husband and son are all buried at St Swithin's, Walcot, Bath. The story of their graves and memorials is an unhappy, as well as a mysterious one, which does not reflect well on the way present-day Bath honours its famous dead.

The 19th century

St Swithin's was not the d'Arblays' place of worship in Bath. As we have seen, Fanny had a seat in the Octagon Chapel, and Alexandre, as a Catholic, probably attended St John's Catholic chapel; certainly Fanny paid for a service of remembrance there for him on the first anniversary of his death, which she did not attend. She had also been scrupulous in permitting a priest to give the last rites on his deathbed. However, St Swithin's was the parish church for almost all of Bath's Georgian expansion north, east and west of the old city. The church had been rebuilt in 1775 to accommodate the growing congregation, but was never adequate to it, nor convenient for most of it, which was why so many proprietary chapels sprang up nearer the fashionable streets. By the turn of the century, indeed, the parish of St Swithin's was the second most populous in England, after that of St Pancras in London. To accommodate all the burials, a cemetery was created on the other side of Walcot Street, much lower down the slope of the hill than the church itself. In 1842, this piece of ground was sanctified by a mortuary chapel, but this of course was after all the d'Arblay burials had taken place.

Alexandre was buried there on 9th May 1818. He would seem to have acceded to his wife's wish of being buried where she could one day join him. He only specified that his funeral be 'simple' and his resting spot be marked by 'merely a tablet of black marble'.

Accordingly the mortuary mason Thomas King of Bath was commissioned by Fanny and her son to produce and erect a black marble polished headstone with an inscription of '23 dozen and

3 letters' engraved and stopped with patent cement, for which a charge of £13.7s.0d. was made. Fanny also ordered King to engrave an elaborate marble tablet to be fixed on the inside wall of the church. (St Swithin's, which has a most attractive Georgian interior, with a gallery round three sides, is replete with these kind of memorials, beautifully executed with bas-relief swags, urns and scrolls; indeed they form its chief decoration and beauty.) Costing a further £33, the tablet recorded Alexandre's honours and virtues at great length:

Sacred to the Memory
of Compte Alexandre Jean Baptiste
PIOCHARD d'ARBLAY;
Chevalier de St. Louis: de la Legion d'Honneur;
du Lys; et de la Fidelite:
Lieutenant General des Armées
et Officier Superieur des Gardes du Corps
de S. M. Louis XVIII, Roi de France.

These Honours, Sole Rewards of his faithful Services,
It is easy to Name, and grateful to Record;
But who shall delineate his noble Character?
The Spirit of his Valour, or the Softness of his Heart?
His feeling Reluctance to leave his weeping Family:
Yet pious Resignation to relinquish this vain World?
His kindness on the Bed of torture:
The *PURITY* of his *INTEGRITY*: the *TRANSPARENCY* of his *HONOUR*;
or the indescribable charm of his Social Virtues?
His shadowy, faded Form
is deposited in *WALCOT* Church Yard.
His devoted Wife, and darling Son
Consecrate This poor Tablet to his loved Remembrance;
With devout Aspiration that his own tender Last prayer
For Their Eternal RE-UNION in the blest Abode
of Immortal Spirits,
May mercifully be accorded
By the ever-living GOD.
Through the mediation of our Lord Jesus Christ. *Amen!*
Died 3d. May, 1818. Aged 65.

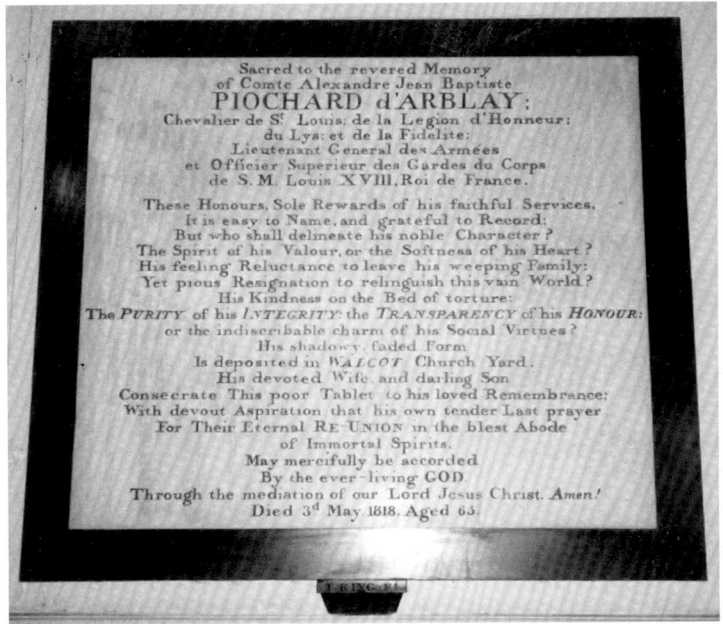

The memorial tablet to Alexandre d'Arblay, in St Swithin's Church

From the point of view of posterity, it is as well that Fanny exceeded her husband's wishes in this way. The tablet may still be seen, but the headstone has gone, leaving Alexandre d'Arblay in an unknown and unmarked grave. But that is only the first disgrace attached to this subject.

As we have seen, Fanny and Alex moved to London after Alexandre's death, and remained there for the rest of their lives. Fanny would never leave London even to visit a sister unless Alex was also away, so convinced was she that he could not manage the practicalities of life without her supervision. He became engaged, but never married, lacking the means and probably the will. Fanny was always worrying that he was too thin, but she never dreamt that he would predecease her. So it was a dreadful shock when on 19th January 1837, just a month after his 42nd birthday, he died suddenly of influenza.

His body was taken back to Bath and buried near that of his father. A headstone must have been made for him, but neither the stone, nor any reference to or record of it exists. The lack of a fulsome tablet, corresponding to that of his father, suggests that Fanny was now too old to summon the energy to compose one. Had she been more capable, it is unlikely she would have been content for Alex to be less honoured than his 15-year-old cousin 'Dolph' Broome, who had died so suddenly in Great Stanhope Street, and whose wall tablet, replete with an 18-line verse specially written by Robert Southey, may still be seen in St Swithin's church.

Three years after her son's death, on 6th January 1840, Fanny herself died, aged 87. Her will specified:

> I desire that wheresoever I may die, my corpse may be conveyed to Bath, there to be interred in like manner with my beloved son's, and as near as possible to my dear and honoured husband's. This is but fulfilling a tender interchange of a promise between the kindest of husbands and myself. I beg that the funeral may be conducted with modest quietness.

The funeral service was conducted by her great-nephew Charles Edward Burney – the fourth Charles in a direct line from her father – and was attended by various members of the family including Sarah Harriet, who was by then the only Burney still living in Bath. Two of her relations travelled from London 'partly by rail-road', thus bringing Fanny Burney's life, which had begun in the reign of George II, right up to the railway age.

Since she was buried in the same grave as her son, it is reasonable to assume that her name was added to his gravestone. In addition, a memorial tablet for the wall of the church was paid for and erected by her heirs and executors. It read:

SACRED TO THE MEMORY OF
FRANCES D'ARBLAY
SECOND DAUGHTER OF CHARLES BURNEY MUS:D:
AND WIDOW OF
GENL. COUNT ALEXANDRE JEAN BAPTISTE PIOCHARD D'ARBLAY,
THE FRIEND OF JOHNSON AND OF BURKE
WHO BY HER TALENTS HAS OBTAINED A NAME
FAR MORE DURABLE THAN MARBLE CAN CONFER.
BY THE PUBLIC SHE WAS ADMIRED FOR HER WRITINGS;
BY THOSE WHO KNEW HER BEST
FOR HER SWEET AND NOBLE DISPOSITION
AND THE BRIGHT EXAMPLE SHE DISPLAYED
OF SELF-DENIAL AND EVERY CHRISTIAN VIRTUE.
BUT HER TRUST WAS PLACED IN GOD
AND HER HOPE RESTED
ON THE MERCY AND MERITS OF HER REDEEEMER
THROUGH WHOM ALONE SHE LOOKED
FOR AN INHERITANCE INCORRUPTIBLE UNDEFILED
AND THAT FADETH NOT AWAY
SHE DIED IN LONDON ON THE 6TH DAY OF JANUARY 1840:
AGED 88.

HER REMAINS ARE DEPOSITED IN THE ADJOINING CHURCH-YARD
NEAR THOSE OF HER BELOVED HUSBAND, AND IN THE SAME
VAULT
WITH THOSE OF HER ONLY SON
THE REVD ALEXANDER CHARLES LOUIS PIOCHARD D'ARBLAY,
WHO DEPARTED THIS LIFE JANUARY 19TH 1837:
AGED 42.

Fanny left all her personal papers to her niece Charlotte Barrett, who was to edit and publish a selection in *The Diary and Letters of Madame d'Arblay*, appearing in seven volumes in the 1840s. Charlotte's son Richard was the main beneficiary of Fanny's will, which included a bequest to her only surviving sister, Sarah Harriet, of £200 per annum. When, four years later, Sarah Harriet died and was buried in Cheltenham, her long association with Bath motivated the family to erect a memorial tablet to her name in St Swithin's church.

The 20th century

To that point, then, the family was well commemorated in Bath. But the first alarm was sounded in 1905, when a bookseller in Bath, J.F. Meehan, published a magazine article deploring the state into which Fanny Burney's grave had been allowed to fall. 'Time has effectually obliterated any inscription there might have been on the stones', he wrote. 'The neglect of man has allowed rank weeds to grow above and around the sacred spot.' He included a photograph of the headstone, an upright white slab, and gave the location as '26^1/$_2$ feet from the south wall, and about 17 ft from the mortuary chapel'.

This and a further article by Clement Shorter, the writer, came to the attention of the man who had buried Fanny 65 years before. Charles Edward Burney was now an Archdeacon, and of course an old man – indeed, he was 90 years of age. His son, the fifth Charles Burney, was despatched to Bath, and a decision made to replace the stone at the family's expense. In September 1906 Clement Shorter was able to write another article congratulating himself on his 'service to literature' and showing the new stone over the caption:

THE NEW MONUMENT OVER THE GRAVE OF FANNY BURNEY
Erected by the family in Walcot Cemetery, Bath, replacing the decayed stone that has covered for more than half-a-century the author of Evelina.

The new stone was nothing like the simple headstones favoured by the d'Arblays themselves. The Edwardian Burneys showed their sense of family honour by commissioning a monumental table-top tomb, estimated to weigh three tons. On the one side were engraved the words:

Sacred to the Memory of
FRANCES D'ARBLAY
Second Daughter of Charles Burney Mus.D.
and Widow of Count Alexandre Piochard D'ARBLAY
who died in London on the 6th day of January 1840
aged 88

and on the other side:

Also of her Son
The Revd ALEXANDER CHARLES L.PIOCHARD
D'ARBLAY
who died January 19th 1837
aged 42

The omission of Fanny's husband from this memorial may or may not suggest that the original black marble stone marking his grave was still in place nearby. What is surely certain is that Fanny herself would have strongly wished all three d'Arblays to be remembered together on such a memorial.

In 1951 the tombstone was photographed, in its position just west of the mortuary chapel, by Professor Joyce Hemlow in the course of her researches for her book *The History of Fanny Burney*. Just four years later, however, the Parochial Church Council of Walcot obtained from the diocesan authorities a faculty permitting them 'to exhume the coffin of the late Fanny Burney … in the Walcot Burial ground for re-interment in a central position in the Churchyard of Walcot St. Swithin and move her Tombstone thereto'. The family was not informed or consulted, though there were then – and are still – many descendants living. It is impossible to recover the motivation of the PCC for this strange act, which involved employing a contractor to move the three-ton stone up hill and across the road to the triangular enclosure formed by the junction, on sharply different levels, of Walcot Street and the London Road.

This is neither as peaceful a spot as the old burial ground, nor as accessible to the interested public, for palings keep them out, and from the traffic-menaced pavement the inscription is illegible. Nor was the action taken strictly in accordance with the terms of the faculty. There is witness to the fact that Fanny's coffin was not exhumed and re-interred, only the stone itself being moved. The consequence is that her body, like that of her husband's, now lies in an unmarked grave.[1]

There is a further mystery. The two memorial tablets to the Burney sisters which were erected by the family inside the church have both disappeared. A photograph of that to Fanny was

[1] All the above information is taken from the final volume (XII) of *The Journals and Letters of Fanny Burney*, edited by Joyce Hemlow, OUP, 1984.

published by Austin Dobson in a biography of 1906, which is how we know its wording, and the tablets remained in place many years after that. The typewritten list of all the memorials in the church which the present verger will produce on request, includes both Fanny's and Sarah Harriet's names. The list is not alphabetical, but is given wall by wall, with the names in the order that the tablets appear. The Burney plaques are both said to be on the west gallery wall. This wall was in fact obscured when an organ was installed in the church in 1958. Nevertheless, it is possible to squeeze between the organ and the wall and to read, with the help of a torch, the wording on the wall tablets. Two blank places, with brackets showing that tablets once were affixed here, occur when the Burney names are reached on the list.

Research in the Somerset Record Office reveals that a faculty to remove these tablets 'to another part of the church' was granted in October 1957 in anticipation of their being obscured by the new organ, the then incumbent being aware of their interest to the public. He was under the erroneous impression that there was no remaining family to consult. But where were the tablets placed? They are certainly not visible in any part of the church today, and nobody presently connected with the church has any knowledge of their removal.[1] It would be wonderful to recover them.

To return to the triangular grassed enclosure left of the church where Fanny's cenotaph (for it is no longer technically her tombstone, having been separated from her remains) now stands. It is a curious coincidence that the only other stone in this area is the slab which once covered the body of Jane Austen's father, the Reverend George Austen, who was buried in the crypt of St Swithin's in January 1805. Like Fanny Burney's, therefore, the exact location of George Austen's grave is now untraceable. The appearance of both stones, carelessly positioned, weatherworn to the point of illegibility and altogether redolent of neglect, is truly dismal, and makes this one of the most poignant corners in Bath. It is one of which the city, so proud of its heritage, so concerned to do the right thing aesthetically, ought really to be ashamed.

[1] I am indebted to Kate Chisholm for drawing my attention to the two tablets to the Burney sisters and for sharing her research, undertaken for the paperback edition of *Fanny Burney, her Life* (see the Bibliography). I am also grateful to her for providing me with a copy of the memorial tablet inscription given on page 89.

The 21st century

Away from Bath, it is gratifying to know that in 2002, the 250th anniversary of her birth, Frances d'Arblay, known to us as Fanny Burney, novelist, playwright and diarist, will be accorded the honour of a plaque in Poet's Corner, Westminster Abbey, London. It is hoped that the century will not pass away without redress to the situation in Bath, the city that she loved in life and looked forward to as her last resting place.

Fanny Burney's tombstone in St Swithin's Churchyard.

Bibliography

The publication history of Fanny Burney's letters and journals is by no means straightforward. Shortly after her death, her niece Charlotte Barrett edited and published a selection in seven volumes, corrupting the text considerably to suit family – and Victorian – sensibilities. She chose to begin her selection in 1778, the date of *Evelina*'s publication, when her aunt's life as a public figure began. In 1889 Annie Raine Ellis brought out an edition of Fanny Burney's pre-*Evelina* diaries, covering the period 1768-78, in two volumes.

Modern scholars have found these early attempts unsatisfactory. Examination of the manuscripts revealed how much was changed from the original, by obliteration or scissors and paste, both by Fanny Burney herself tampering in her old age, and by her niece. Professor Joyce Hemlow, having written her masterly *History of Fanny Burney*, set out to decipher and transcribe the original text. Between 1972 and 1984, she brought out a twelve-volume scholarly edition, but for various reasons this did not begin until Fanny's release from court in the summer of 1791 (just two weeks before her third visit to Bath described in the present Chapter 3).

Professor Hemlow's work is now being completed by a team at McGill University, Montreal, where a substantial proportion of Burney papers, together with copies of papers belonging to other institutions, are housed. Under the direction of Professor Lars Troide, it is planned to publish a further twelve volumes covering the period March 1768 to July 1791. Thus eventually it is hoped that there will be a full scholarly edition, running to twenty-four volumes, covering Fanny's life from March 1768 when she began to keep a diary, to her death in January 1840. To date, the first three volumes have appeared, reaching to 1778, while the fourth, which will cover the second Bath visit of 1780 (the subject of my Chapter 2) is in the press. That I was able to work from the most recent edition of the 1780 journal is thanks to Dr Stuart Cooke, of the Burney project at McGill, who kindly transmitted the text to me electronically before publication.

All quotations in this book, unless otherwise annotated, have been taken from these sources.

Readers inspired to delve more extensively in the letters and diaries should therefore consult:

For 1768-1778
The Early Journals and Letters of Fanny Burney, 1768-91,
> edited by Lars Troide *et al.* (twelve volumes, of which only three are yet published, Oxford University Press, 1988-94)

For 1779-July 1791 (until the above sequence is complete)
The Diary & Letters of Madame d'Arblay, 1778-1840,
> edited by her niece Charlotte Barrett (seven volumes, London, 1842-46)

For August 1791-1840
The Journals and Letters of Fanny Burney (Madame d'Arblay), 1791-1840,
> edited by Joyce Hemlow *et al.* (twelve volumes, Oxford University Press, 1972-84)

Fanny Burney's novels, with date of first publication are:
Evelina; or the History of a Young Lady's Entrance into the World, 1778
Cecilia; or Memoirs of an Heiress, 1782
Camilla; or a Picture of Youth, 1796
The Wanderer; or Female Difficulties, 1814
All are available in the World's Classics series from Oxford University Press, with annotations and introductions by present-day scholars.

Fanny Burney's collected plays are now also available in a modern scholarly edition:
The Complete Plays of Frances Burney:
Volume I: Comedies (including *A Busy Day* and *The Witlings*);
Volume II: Tragedies; both volumes edited by Peter Sabor, Stuart J. Cooke *et al.*, (Pickering, 1995)

Biographies of Fanny Burney which I recommend include, in chronological order of publication:
Hemlow, Joyce, *A History of Fanny Burney*, Oxford University Press, 1958
Doody, Margaret Anne, *Frances Burney, the Life in the Works*, Cambridge University Press, 1988
Chisholm, Kate, *Fanny Burney, her Life*, Chatto & Windus, 1998

Studies of Bath which I have found useful in supplying background material for this book are:

Gadd, David, *Georgian Summer: Bath in the Eighteenth Century*, Adams & Dart, 1971

Hill, Mary K., *Bath and the Eighteenth Century Novel*, Bath University Press, 1989

Ison, Walter, *The Georgian Buildings of Bath*, Faber & Faber, 1948, reprinted Kingsmead Press, 1969

Neale, R.S., *Bath 1680-1850, A Social History*, Routledge & Kegan Paul, 1981

Cover illustration: South Parade, Bath by Thomas Malton, 1778. (Reproduced by courtesy of Victoria Art Gallery, Bath & North East Somerset)